The Good Working Life

"This exciting new book covers Zacher's pioneering research that applies grand theories about the good life to the everyday activity of work. Drawing on diverse sources, ranging from ancient Greek philosophy to the latest scientific data, the book rapidly moves beyond the simple issue of job satisfaction to address two other key questions: What makes a job meaningful? And what enables work to provide interesting, psychologically rich experiences? Perhaps surprisingly, the answers are quite similar across many different kinds of people—yet the outcomes differ dramatically by occupation. Whether you are a young worker trying to choose a line of work, or a senior manager seeking to design a workplace that will engage employees better, this book is an essential read."

—Roy F. Baumeister, *Harvard University*

Hannes Zacher

The Good Working Life

Experiencing Satisfaction, Meaningfulness, and Psychological Richness in Organizations

palgrave
macmillan

Hannes Zacher
Wilhelm Wundt Institute of Psychology
Leipzig University
Leipzig, Sachsen, Germany

ISBN 978-3-031-77220-7 ISBN 978-3-031-77221-4 (eBook)
https://doi.org/10.1007/978-3-031-77221-4

This Palgrave Macmillan imprint is published by the registered company Springer Nature Switzerland AG.
The registered company address is: Gewerbestrasse 11, 6330 Cham, Switzerland

For Megan. To the good life, in all its splendor!

Acknowledgments

The author acknowledges the support of Leipzig University and the Volkswagen Foundation (Az. 96 849, "The Role of Work in the Development of Civilization Diseases" and Az. 96 849-1, "Work and Health in the Time of COVID-19: A Longitudinal Study").

Competing Interests The author has no financial or non-financial conflicts of interest in relation to the content of this book.

Ethics Approval All research reported in this book that involved human participants was performed in accordance with the ethical standards of the institutional and national research committees and with the 1964 Helsinki Declaration and its later amendments or comparable ethical standards. Participation in the studies was voluntary, and data were saved and processed anonymously. Informed consent about participation and publication was obtained from all participants included in the studies.

Contents

About the Author

Hannes Zacher is a Professor of Work and Organizational Psychology at the Wilhelm Wundt Institute of Psychology at Leipzig University in Germany. He studied psychology at the undergraduate and postgraduate levels at the Technical University of Braunschweig and the University of Minnesota. In 2009, he earned his Ph.D. from the University of Giessen and subsequently worked in academic positions in Germany, Australia, and the Netherlands. In his research program, Hannes investigates aging at work and career development, occupational health and well-being, proactive and adaptive employee behavior, and organizational environmental sustainability. Across these research agendas, he employs multiple methodologies, including experimental, longitudinal, experience sampling, and meta-analytic studies. His research is well supported through competitive grants and industry funding. Hannes has published eight books, more than 70 book chapters, and over 200 articles in peer-reviewed academic journals. He also serves on the editorial boards of several international journals. Since 2024, Hannes has been the Editor-in-Chief of *Psychology and Aging*, the premier outlet for the psychological science of aging and adult lifespan development published by the American Psychological Association. He lives with his wife and their four children in Leipzig, Germany.

List of Figures

List of Tables

CHAPTER 1

Introduction

Abstract Based on the ancient philosophical notion of "the good life" and its modern adaptations in the discipline of psychological science, in this chapter, I introduce the concept of "the good working life." The good working life entails a combination of high levels of job satisfaction, work meaningfulness, and work psychological richness. As a guide for subsequent chapters of this book, I present a theoretical model of potential antecedents and consequences of the good working life, including individual and work characteristics, as well as work and life outcomes. Moreover, I introduce a large-scale empirical survey study with over 2000 workers conducted for this book to obtain an evidence-based understanding of the good working life. The methods and results of this study are described in the subsequent chapters of this book.

Keywords The good life • Happiness • Life satisfaction • Meaning in life • Psychological richness

"What constitutes a good life?" This question is one of the oldest questions philosophers have attempted to answer. Aristippus (435–356 BC) proposed that the experience of pleasure and joy is the ultimate goal in life. In contrast, Aristotle (384–322 BC) argued in his *Nicomachean Ethics* that humans should strive toward a contemplative and virtuous life. He

H. Zacher, *The Good Working Life*,
https://doi.org/10.1007/978-3-031-77221-4_1

conceived such a life as filled with reflective and honorable activities, including intellectual and political pursuits. In contrast, Aristotle frowned upon a hedonistic life full of lust, pleasure, and money-making. Based on this ancient tradition, the discipline of psychological science has conceptualized "the good life" in terms of hedonic well-being (or subjective well-being; e.g., happiness, life satisfaction, the experience of many positive and few negative emotions; Diener, 1984; Diener, 2000) and eudaimonic well-being (or psychological well-being; e.g., experienced meaningfulness, purpose in life, personal growth; Ryan & Deci, 2001; Ryff, 1989).

Research has shown that hedonic and eudaimonic well-being overlap substantially but represent distinct domains of human well-being (Chen et al., 2013). People who live a happy life are also more likely to live a meaningful life, and vice versa. At the same time, a study by Baumeister et al. (2013) showed that happiness and meaningfulness can be distinguished. When statistically controlling for meaningfulness, happiness had unique and differential associations with other variables compared to meaningfulness (e.g., satisfying one's needs and wants, being a taker). Likewise, when controlling for happiness, meaningfulness was related to other variables apart from happiness (e.g., concerns with personal identity and expressing the self, being a giver).

More recently, the traditional two-dimensional conceptualization of the good life in terms of hedonic and eudaimonic well-being was extended to include the concept of "psychological richness." According to Oishi and colleagues, a psychologically rich life provides a variety of interesting, complex, emotionally intense, and perspective-changing experiences (Besser & Oishi, 2020; Oishi et al., 2020). The psychologically rich life thus differs conceptually from the happy life, which is characterized by comfort, joy, and security, and the meaningful life, which is characterized by significance, purpose, and coherence (Oishi & Westgate, 2022). Oishi and colleagues also demonstrated empirically that psychological richness is distinct from hedonic and eudaimonic well-being and has unique associations with other variables. Moreover, Oishi and Westgate (2022) reported that "a nontrivial number of people around the world report they would choose a psychologically rich life at the expense of a happy or meaningful life" (p. 790). Table 1.1 summarizes the three dimensions of the good life and their definitions.

Numerous studies in the discipline of psychological science have examined antecedents and consequences of the good life in general—conceptualized in terms of hedonic and eudaimonic well-being (for reviews, see

Table 1.1 Definitions of the three dimensions of the good life

Dimension	*Definition*
Hedonic well-being (also called subjective well-being or happiness)	"A broad category of phenomena that includes people's emotional responses (i.e., pleasant and unpleasant affect, such as joy and sadness, respectively), domain satisfactions (e.g., work, family), and global judgments of life satisfaction" (Diener, 1984, p. 277).
Eudaimonic well-being (also called psychological well-being or meaningfulness)	"Striving toward excellence based on one's unique potential" (Ryff & Singer, 2008, p. 14), including purpose in life, environmental mastery, positive relationships, personal growth, autonomy, and self-acceptance (Ryff, 1995).
Psychological richness	Living a life "characterized by variety, interestingness, and perspective change" (Oishi & Westgate, 2022, p. 4).

Diener, 2018; Kesebir & Diener, 2008; King & Hicks, 2021). In contrast, the tripartite conceptualization, including satisfaction, meaningfulness, and psychological richness, has only recently been applied to the context of paid work and employment, which represents one of the most important domains or roles in many people's lives. Using survey data from 678 workers in different jobs, organizations, and occupations, Zacher and Baumeister (2024) examined unique (i.e., statistically controlling for the respective other two dimensions) and differential associations between each of three dimensions of "the good working life" (i.e., job satisfaction, work meaningfulness, and work psychological richness), multiple work characteristics, and several important work and life outcomes. The results of this initial study on the good working life are described in detail in the next chapter.

Consistent with the evidence-based notion that "bad is stronger than good" (Baumeister et al., 2001), most research in the area of work and organizational psychology has focused on negative aspects of people's working lives, such as stress, conflicts, poor performance, and quitting. In the spirit of a more positive psychology in general and a positive organizational psychology specifically (Niessen & Zacher, 2023; Seligman & Csikszentmihalyi, 2000), I believe it is time to focus on people's positive work experiences, as well as the antecedents and consequences of such experiences. Accordingly, the overarching goal of this book is to build on the initial study on the good working life by Zacher and Baumeister (2024) by obtaining a more comprehensive, evidence-based understanding of this concept. Based on a large-scale survey study conducted for this book, including over 2000 workers from various jobs, organizations, and occupations in Germany, I demonstrate how the three dimensions of the good working life are uniquely and differentially related to various individual and work characteristics, as well as several important work and life outcomes.

Theoretical Model

The theoretical model guiding the investigation of the good working life in this book is shown in Fig. 1.1. The conceptualization and measurement of the good working life are described in further detail in Chaps. 2 and 3, respectively. As potential antecedents of the three good working life dimensions, I examine various individual characteristics in Chap. 4, including demographic characteristics (e.g., age, sex, education) and personality characteristics (e.g., Big Five characteristics, psychological capital, dark triad traits), as well as the use of character strengths (i.e., positive, morally desirable, and virtuous characteristics) and job crafting behaviors (i.e., workers' proactive efforts to improve the fit between their abilities and needs and their job demands and resources, respectively). In Chap. 5, I explore relations between the three dimensions of the good working life and several work characteristics, including employment characteristics (e.g., industry) and job characteristics. Regarding the latter, in an effort to replicate and extend the initial study by Zacher and Baumeister (2024), I

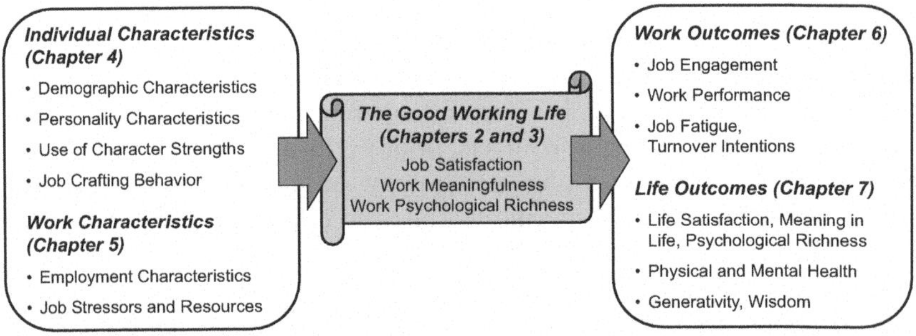

Fig. 1.1 Theoretical model with potential antecedents and consequences of the good working life

examine several important job stressors (e.g., emotional job demands) and job resources (e.g., opportunities for development).

Turning to the potential consequences of the good working life, in Chaps. 6 and 7, I investigate several key work outcomes (e.g., job engagement, work performance, job fatigue) and several important life outcomes (e.g., life satisfaction, physical and mental health), respectively. The investigation of these broader work and life outcomes of the good working life also replicates and extends the initial work by Zacher and Baumeister (2024). Finally, Chap. 8 concludes the book with a summary of 15 key insights gained in the preceding chapters, as well as several recommendations for future research and practical implications regarding the good working life.

Empirical Study

To empirically examine the relations between the three dimensions of the good working life and their potential antecedents and consequences proposed in the theoretical model (Fig. 1.1), I collected data from a large sample of workers in Germany at two measurement waves six months apart (i.e., Time 1 at the beginning of December 2023 and Time 2 at the beginning of June 2024). The focus of this book is on the relations between the good working life and other variables collected at Time 1, but I also report some relations between the good working life and other variables that were only collected at Time 2. I commissioned a professional online panel company to recruit and incentivize employed participants from a nationally representative online panel in Germany. The company is ISO 26362 certified, which ensures quality of the data. Participation in the study was voluntary and anonymous, and informed written consent about participation and publication of the research was obtained from all individuals prior to the commencement of the study. At Time 1, the survey was initiated by 2280 individuals, and 2030 workers completed the survey. At Time 2, the survey was initiated by 1353 of the same workers who participated at Time 1, and 1325 workers completed the Time 2 survey.

The descriptive statistics for participants' demographic and employment characteristics collected at Time 1 are presented in Table 1.2. Workers' ages ranged from 19 to 70 years, with an average age of approximately 43 years, which is comparable to the average age of the working population in Germany in the year 2024. Approximately half of the

Table 1.2 Summary of participant demographic and employment characteristics ($N = 2030$)

Participant characteristics	*Descriptive statistics*
Demographic characteristics	
Age (years)	
Mean (SD)	43.4 (13.0)
Median [min, max]	43.0 [19, 70]
Sex	
Male	52.4%
Female	47.5%
Diverse	0.001%
Highest level of education	
No school degree	0.001%
Lower secondary school	5.8%
Intermediate secondary school	30.2%
Upper secondary school	26.7%
College/university or technical college	37.3%
Nationality	
German	97.9%
Other	2.1%
Migration background	
No	92.7%
Yes	7.3%
Employment characteristics	
Job level (1 = *entry level*, 7 = *executive position*)	
Mean (SD)	4.1 (1.38)
Median [min, max]	4.0 [1, 7]
Income (Euro)	
Mean (SD)	2844.6 (1532.9)
Median [min, max]	2500.0 [1000, 20,000]
Financial difficulties (1 = *never*, 5 = *always*)	
Mean (SD)	1.8 (1.1)
Median [min, max]	1.0 [1, 5]
Industry	
Primary sector (extraction of raw materials)	0.01%
Secondary sector (manufacturing)	20.8%
Tertiary sector (service)	78.2%
Supervisory status	
No	69.7%
Yes	30.1%

(*continued*)

Table 1.2 (continued)

Participant characteristics	*Descriptive statistics*
Work hours	
Mean (SD)	41.2 (6.0)
Median [min, max]	40.0 [20, 80]
Shift work	
Day work	86.2%
Shift work	13.8%
Contract type	
Permanent employment	93.8%
Temporary employment	6.2%
Working from home (% of working time per week)	
Mean (SD)	23.0 (29.8)
Median [min, max]	5.0 [0, 100]

Note: SD = standard deviation, min = minimum value, max = maximum value

participants were men (52.4%), and the other half were women (47.5%; two individuals identified as diverse). In terms of the highest level of education, a majority of participants held an intermediate secondary school degree (30.2%), an upper secondary school degree (26.7%), or a degree from a technical college, college, or university (37.3%). The vast majority of participants had a German passport (97.9%); the other 2.1% of participants also lived in Germany at the time of the study but originally came from Afghanistan, Albania, Austria, Belgium, Bosnia, Bulgaria, China, Croatia, France, Greece, Hungary, Iran, United Kingdom, Latvia, the Netherlands, Russia, Spain, South Africa, or Ukraine. A migration background (i.e., either the participant or at least one of their parents was not born in Germany) was reported by 7.3% of participants.

In terms of employment characteristics, workers' job level ranged from entry level to executive positions, with a mean of 4.1 on a 7-point scale. The mean monthly net income was 2845 Euros, and the median monthly net income of participants was 2500 Euros. These values are slightly higher than the mean monthly net income (2741 Euros) and the median monthly net income (2443 Euro) of the employed population in Germany in 2024. Accordingly, most participants in the study did not report having difficulties buying groceries or paying their rent and bills (mean of 1.8 on a 5-point scale). The majority of participants worked in the service industry (i.e., tertiary sector; 78.2%), whereas only 20.8% worked in an agricultural job (i.e., primary sector) or a manufacturing job (i.e., secondary sector). These statistics are largely consistent with the employed population in Germany in 2024 (i.e., 75.3% tertiary, 23.5% secondary, 1.2% primary). The distribution of participants across specific industries and differences in the good working life across these industries are presented in Chap. 5.

Most participants did not have supervisory responsibilities (69.7%) and worked in a day job (86.2%), whereas only 13.8% worked according to a shift work schedule. These statistics also correspond to those for the employed population in Germany, where 14.8% of all employees work according to a shift schedule. Most participants had a permanent work contract (93.8%), whereas only 6.2% of workers were in temporary employment. These statistics correspond to the employed population in Germany in 2024, where 7.5% of all workers were in temporary employment. Finally, the mean percentage of time working from home per week was 23% (i.e., approximately two days per week); however, most participants indicated that they never worked from home. After the COVID-19 pandemic, which started in March 2020 and was declared over in May 2023 by the World Health Organization (Zacher & Rudolph, 2024), workers in many industries regularly worked from home for at least one day per week (Rudolph & Zacher, 2024).

Participants in the study conducted for this book came from a broad variety of jobs. Figure 1.2 shows a word cloud of 200 representative job titles of workers who participated in the study. Common job titles of participants included accountant, administrative worker, architect, call center agent, chemical laboratory technician, computer scientist, controller, cook, customer service representative, dispatcher, engineer, factory worker, geriatric nurse, human resources officer, insurance agent, IT specialist, logistics employee, manager, nurse, office clerk, police officer, project manager, salesperson, secretary, security guard, service staff, social worker, software developer, teacher, technician, and warehouse worker.

Less common job titles provided by participants included air cargo handler, art director, attorney, baker, bricklayer, bus driver, butcher, carpenter, construction worker, correctional officer, credit analyst, delivery driver, dental assistant, designer, driving instructor, educator, electrical engineer, electrician, emergency paramedic, event manager, executive assistant, facility manager, farmer, fitter, flight attendant, florist, food inspector, forklift driver, fruit seller, gallery owner, garbage collector, gardener, graphic designer, health economist, horse riding teacher, hotel

Fig. 1.2 Selection of 200 representative job titles of workers who participated in the study

manager, industrial mechanic, integration officer, intensive care nurse, interior designer, journalist, judge, laboratory technician, lawyer, lecturer, legal assistant, librarian, lifeguard, locksmith, machine operator, masseur, mechanical engineer, media designer, money courier, music producer, operations manager, occupational therapist, optician, painter, paramedic, pharmaceutical technical assistant, physiotherapist, piano teacher, postal worker, professor, real estate agent, receptionist, registrar, restaurant manager, roofer, soldier, speaker, speech therapist, surgeon, swimming instructor, tour guide, train driver, travel agent, truck driver, undertaker, veterinarian, waiter, and web designer.

Summary

The ancient philosophical notion of "the good life" has traditionally been conceptualized and operationalized in modern psychological science as hedonic well-being (e.g., life satisfaction) and eudaimonic well-being (e.g., meaningfulness). Hedonic and eudaimonic well-being are strongly and positively related but represent distinct concepts with unique antecedents and consequences. Based on recent theoretical developments in the psychology of human well-being, the notion of the good working life can be conceptualized and operationalized as a combination of high levels of job satisfaction, work meaningfulness, and work psychological richness. Potential antecedents of the good working life include various individual and work characteristics, and its potential consequences include several important work and life outcomes. To obtain a more comprehensive and evidence-based understanding of the good working life, I conducted a large-scale survey study with over 2000 workers in Germany. The results of this empirical study are described in the subsequent chapters of this book.

References

Baumeister, R. F., Bratslavsky, E., Finkenauer, C., & Vohs, K. D. (2001). Bad is stronger than good. *Review of General Psychology, 5*(4), 323–370. https://doi.org/10.1037/1089-2680.5.4.323

Baumeister, R. F., Vohs, K. D., Aaker, J. L., & Garbinsky, E. N. (2013). Some key differences between a happy life and a meaningful life. *Journal of Positive Psychology, 8*(6), 505–516. https://doi.org/10.1080/17439760.2013.830764

Besser, L. L., & Oishi, S. (2020). The psychologically rich life. *Philosophical Psychology, 33*(8), 1053–1071. https://doi.org/10.1080/09515089.2020.1778662

Chen, F. F., Jing, Y., Hayes, A., & Lee, J. M. (2013). Two concepts or two approaches? A bifactor analysis of psychological and subjective well-being. *Journal of Happiness Studies, 14*, 1033–1068. https://doi.org/10.1007/s10902-012-9367-x

Diener, E. (1984). Subjective well-being. *Psychological Bulletin, 95*(3), 542–575. https://doi.org/10.1037/0033-2909.95.3.542

Diener, E. (2000). Subjective well-being: The science of happiness and a proposal for a national index. *American Psychologist, 55*(1), 34–43. https://doi.org/10.1037/0003-066X.55.1.34

Diener, E. (2018). Happiness: The science of subjective well-being. In R. Biswas-Diener & E. Diener (Eds.), *Noba textbook series: Psychology*. DEF.

Kesebir, P., & Diener, E. (2008). In pursuit of happiness: Empirical answers to philosophical questions. *Perspectives on Psychological Science, 3*(2), 117–125. https://doi.org/10.1111/j.1745-6916.2008.00069.x

King, L. A., & Hicks, J. A. (2021). The science of meaning in life. *Annual Review of Psychology, 72*, 561–584. https://doi.org/10.1146/annurev-psych-072420-122921

Niessen, C., & Zacher, H. (2023). Positive organizational psychology. In H. Zacher & N. Lehmann-Willenbrock (Eds.), *Work, organizational, and business psychology: An introductory textbook* (pp. 165–183). Kohlhammer.

Oishi, S., Choi, H., Koo, M., Galinha, I., Ishii, K., Komiya, A., et al. (2020). Happiness, meaning, and psychological richness. *Affective Science, 1*, 107–115. https://doi.org/10.1007/s42761-020-00011-z

Oishi, S., & Westgate, E. C. (2022). A psychologically rich life: Beyond happiness and meaning. *Psychological Review, 129*(4), 790–811. https://doi.org/10.1037/rev0000317

Rudolph, C. W., & Zacher, H. (2024). Working from home: When is it too much of a good thing? *Human Resource Development Quarterly*. https://doi.org/10.1002/hrdq.21530

Ryan, R. M., & Deci, E. L. (2001). On happiness and human potentials: A review of research on hedonic and eudaimonic well-being. *Annual Review of Psychology, 52*(1), 141–166. https://doi.org/10.1146/annurev.psych.52.1.141

Ryff, C. D. (1989). Happiness is everything, or is it? Explorations on the meaning of psychological well-being. *Journal of Personality and Social Psychology, 57*(6), 1069–1081. https://doi.org/10.1037/0022-3514.57.6.1069

Ryff, C. D. (1995). Psychological well-being in adult life. *Current Directions in Psychological Science, 4*(4), 99–104. https://doi.org/10.1111/1467-8721.ep10772395

Ryff, C. D., & Singer, B. H. (2008). Know thyself and become what you are: A eudaimonic approach to psychological well-being. *Journal of Happiness Studies, 9*(1), 13–39. https://doi.org/10.1007/s10902-006-9019-0

Seligman, M. E., & Csikszentmihalyi, M. (2000). Positive psychology: An introduction. *American Psychologist, 55*(1), 5–14. https://doi.org/10.1037/0003-066X.55.1.5

Zacher, H., & Baumeister, R. F. (2024). Differences among a satisfied, a meaningful, and a psychologically rich working life. *Journal of Positive Psychology*. https://doi.org/10.1080/17439760.2024.2417102

Zacher, H., & Rudolph, C. W. (2024). Subjective wellbeing during the COVID-19 pandemic: A 3-year, 35-wave longitudinal study. *Journal of Positive Psychology, 19*(3), 442–456. https://doi.org/10.1080/17439760.2023.2224757

CHAPTER 2

The Good Working Life

Abstract In this chapter, I define and explain the three dimensions of the good working life, including job satisfaction, work meaningfulness, and work psychological richness. Job satisfaction refers to a positive, pleasurable emotional state that results from the evaluation of one's job and job-related experiences. Work meaningfulness involves people's belief that their work is important and has a growth- and purpose-oriented focus. Work psychological richness refers to people's experience that their working life is characterized by complexity, entails a variety of interesting and perspective-changing experiences, and involves feeling a variety of deep emotions. I describe the results of previous research on the potential antecedents and consequences of these three dimensions of the good working life. Additionally, I present novel findings on which kind of working life—a satisfied, a meaningful, or a psychologically rich working life—people would choose for themselves if they could only pick one of these options.

Keywords The good working life • Job satisfaction • Work meaningfulness • Work psychological richness

Based on the ancient philosophical notion of the good life and modern adaptations and extensions of the concept in psychological science, the good working life can be represented by three interrelated yet distinct

H. Zacher, *The Good Working Life*,
https://doi.org/10.1007/978-3-031-77221-4_2

Table 2.1 Definitions of the three dimensions of the good working life

Dimension	*Definition*
Job satisfaction	"A pleasurable or positive emotional state resulting from the appraisal of one's job or job experiences" (Locke, 1976, p. 1304).
Work meaningfulness	People's belief that their work "is both significant and positive in valence ... the positive valence of MW [meaningful work] has a eudaimonic (growth- and purpose-oriented) rather than hedonic (pleasure-oriented) focus" (Steger et al., 2012, p. 323). Three dimensions of a higher-order work meaningfulness construct: (a) Personal meaning in work (i.e., "the sense that people judge their work to matter and be meaningful"), (b) Meaning making through work (i.e., people's perception that their work helps them "deepen their understanding of their selves and the world around them, facilitating their personal growth"), and (c) Greater good motivations (i.e., the belief that one's work "make[s] a positive impact on the greater good"; Steger et al., 2012, pp. 324–325).
Work psychological richness	People's experience that their working life is characterized by complexity entails a variety of interesting and perspective-changing experiences and involves feeling a variety of deep emotions (Besser & Oishi, 2020; Zacher & Baumeister, 2024).

dimensions: job satisfaction, work meaningfulness, and work psychological richness (Zacher & Baumeister, 2024). Table 2.1 summarizes these dimensions and their definitions. Consistent with psychological theorizing on human well-being in general (e.g., Ryan & Deci, 2001), Sonnentag (2015) describes workers' experiences of hedonic and eudaimonic well-being as two overarching dimensions of *occupational* well-being. Accordingly, Zacher and Baumeister (2024) included a prominent indicator of each of these two dimensions—job satisfaction and work meaningfulness—in their conceptualization of the good working life. Additionally, based on theoretical advances by Oishi and colleagues (e.g., Besser & Oishi, 2020; Oishi & Westgate, 2022), they included work psychological richness as a third and novel dimension of occupational well-being to form a tripartite conceptualization of the good working life. In this book, I also use this conceptualization proposed by Zacher and Baumeister (2024).

Job Satisfaction

Job satisfaction is a core indicator of hedonic well-being or happiness at work (Judge & Klinger, 2008; Schmitt et al., 2012). It can be defined as a cognitive-affective construct representing "a pleasurable or positive emotional state resulting from the appraisal of one's job or job experiences" (Locke, 1976, p. 1304). Thus, job satisfaction entails the frequent experience of positive emotions at work (e.g., enthusiasm, cheerfulness, contentment) and the infrequent experience of negative emotions at work (e.g., anger, sadness, frustration; Weiss & Cropanzano, 1996). Numerous empirical studies have examined individual characteristics (e.g., personality) and work characteristics (e.g., job autonomy) as potential antecedents of job satisfaction, as well as various potential outcomes of job satisfaction (e.g., performance, withdrawal behavior; Harrison et al., 2006; Judge & Kammeyer-Mueller, 2012; Judge et al., 2017).

The goal of the empirical study conducted for this book was to examine antecedents and consequences of job satisfaction similar to those in previous research. However, the study extends previous research by exploring unique associations between job satisfaction and its potential antecedents and consequences by controlling for the other two dimensions of the good working life (i.e., work meaningfulness and work psychological richness).

Work Meaningfulness

Work meaningfulness is a principal indicator of eudaimonic well-being in the work context (Barrick et al., 2013; Blustein et al., 2023). The construct involves people's belief that their work is significant and important and that their work has a growth- and purpose-oriented focus (Steger et al., 2012). In their initial study on the good working life, Zacher and Baumeister (2024) examined work meaningfulness in terms of people's perception that their work makes important contributions to other people and society (see Bunderson & Thompson, 2009). In this book, I include this facet of work meaningfulness as part of a more comprehensive conceptualization of work meaningfulness. Specifically, following Steger et al. (2012), I conceptualize and operationalize work meaningfulness in terms of three facets: (a) personal meaning in work (i.e., "the sense that people judge their work to matter and be meaningful"), (b) meaning making through work (i.e., people's perception that their work helps them "deepen their understanding of their selves and the world around them, facilitating their personal growth"), and (c) greater good motivations (i.e., the belief that one's work "make[s] a positive impact on the greater good" (Steger et al., 2012, pp. 324–325).

Zacher and Baumeister (2024) measured only the greater good motivation facet of work meaningfulness in their initial study on the good working life, whereas they did not include the closely related facets of personal meaning in work and meaning making through work. In this book, I extend the earlier work by conceptualizing and measuring work meaningfulness as a broader construct. Just like happiness and experienced meaningfulness in life are positively related but distinct constructs (Baumeister et al., 2013), research has shown that job satisfaction and work meaningfulness are positively related yet distinct (Duffy et al., 2015). Additionally, research has identified various sources of work meaningfulness, including personal values and beliefs, work characteristics, and national culture (Rosso et al., 2010). Moreover, a meta-analysis reported associations between work meaningfulness and several important outcomes, including job engagement, self-rated job performance, (lower) withdrawal intentions, life satisfaction, and health (Allan et al., 2019).

As for job satisfaction, I examine similar antecedents and consequences of work meaningfulness in the empirical study conducted for this book. Extending previous research, however, I explore the unique associations between work meaningfulness and its potential antecedents and consequences by controlling for the other two dimensions of the good working life (i.e., job satisfaction and work psychological richness).

Work Psychological Richness

Work psychological richness constitutes the third core dimension of the good working life and occupational well-being. It was adapted by Zacher and Baumeister (2024) from the broader notion of psychological richness in life in general (Oishi & Westgate, 2022). Based on the work of Oishi and colleagues, work psychological richness is defined as people's experience that their working life is characterized by complexity, entails a variety of interesting and perspective-changing experiences, and involves feeling a variety of deep emotions (Besser & Oishi, 2020; Zacher & Baumeister, 2024). In their research, Oishi and colleagues showed that psychological richness is positively related to, but distinct from, hedonic and eudaimonic forms of well-being. For example, they found that higher curiosity, more holistic thinking, and a more liberal political orientation are associated with the experience of a psychologically rich life (Oishi & Westgate, 2022). Moreover, studying abroad, which represents a rather unusual life experience among citizens of the United States, has been shown to be positively associated with psychological richness but not with life satisfaction and meaning in life (Oishi et al., 2021).

In the empirical study conducted for this book, I examine the same sets of potential antecedents and consequences of job satisfaction and work meaningfulness in relation to work psychological richness. Importantly, the focus here is again on the unique associations between work psychological richness and its potential antecedents and consequences after controlling for the other two dimensions of the good working life (i.e., job satisfaction and work meaningfulness).

Previous Research on the Good Working Life

The first empirical study on the good working life was accepted for publication in the *Journal of Positive Psychology* in 2024 (Zacher & Baumeister, 2024). Based on previous research on relations between happiness and meaningfulness in general (Baumeister et al., 2013), the researchers expected that job satisfaction, work meaningfulness, and work psychological richness would also overlap substantially. Indeed, they found strong and positive correlations among the three dimensions of the good working life. Based on previous research by Baumeister et al. (2013), as well as various theories on job characteristics and important work and life outcomes, they further expected that the three dimensions of the good working life would have unique and differential associations with the potential antecedents (i.e., job stressors and job resources) and consequences (i.e., various work and life outcomes) assessed in their study.

Zacher and Baumeister (2024) found that *the satisfied working life* was associated with comparatively low levels of key job stressors, including qualitative and quantitative workload, work interruptions, environmental stressors (e.g., heat, noise), supervisor and coworker undermining, and job insecurity. In contrast, workers who were satisfied with their job reported consistently higher levels of job resources, including job autonomy, skill variety, perceived contribution to a complete work process (also called task identity), participation, development opportunities, supervisor and coworker support, perceived organizational support, job level, and percentage of working from home. Additionally, the satisfied working life was linked to several favorable work and life outcomes, including higher job proficiency, work ability, job engagement, work-family balance satisfaction and perceived effectiveness, physical and mental health, and family and life satisfaction. Surprisingly, job adaptivity was not significantly related to the satisfied working life, and job proactivity was negatively related to it. A possible explanation for these findings is that showing high levels of adaptivity and proactivity on the job is not always pleasant undertakings but can go along with various negative emotions and strain. Finally, consistent with expectations, the satisfied working life related negatively to several unfavorable work outcomes, such that workers who experienced high levels of job satisfaction also experienced lower levels of job fatigue, turnover intentions, sickness absenteeism and presenteeism, and financial difficulties.

The *meaningful working life* demonstrated a mixed pattern of results in the initial study on the good working life (Zacher & Baumeister, 2024). Most work stressors were unrelated to the meaningful working life. Exceptions were qualitative and quantitative workload and working hours, which were weakly and positively correlated with work meaningfulness: Workers who reported higher work meaningfulness also had a higher workload and longer working hours. Likewise, the work resources' perceived contribution, participation, development opportunities, as well as supervisor and coworker support were weakly and positively related to the meaningful working life. Furthermore, work meaningfulness was positively, albeit again weakly, associated with most, but not all, work and life outcomes, such that the meaningful working life was linked to higher job proficiency, adaptivity, and proactivity, as well as higher work ability, job engagement, and family and life satisfaction. Work meaningfulness was also associated with slightly reduced turnover intentions and sickness absenteeism. Overall, in contrast to the satisfied working life, the meaningful working life was more difficult to pin down in Zacher and Baumeister's (2024) initial study, possibly because the researchers focused only on one aspect of meaningful work: the perceived importance of one's job to other people and society (Bunderson & Thompson, 2009). In the study conducted for this book, I examine a broader conceptualization of work meaningfulness that includes not only greater good motivations but also personal meaning in work and meaning making through work (Steger et al., 2012).

The *psychologically rich working life*, similar to the satisfied and meaningful working lives, was also associated with higher levels in most job resources, with the exceptions of perceived organizational support and working from home (presumably because working in one's home environment offers less stimulation than the traditional workplace). Interestingly, all of the job stressors investigated, with the exception of working hours, contributed to a more psychologically rich working life. Specifically, workers who reported higher psychological richness at work also experienced a higher workload, as well as more interruptions, environmental stressors, supervisor and coworker undermining, and job insecurity. The psychologically rich working life was also a double-edged sword regarding most of the work and life outcomes investigated. Although people with a psychologically rich working life reported higher levels of job adaptivity, proactivity, and engagement, they also reported somewhat lower physical and mental health, as well as more job fatigue, turnover intentions, sickness presenteeism, and financial difficulties than people without a psychologically rich working life.

Overall, Zacher and Baumeister's (2024) initial study offers several interesting insights into the unique association between the three dimensions of the good working life and various potential antecedents and consequences. In the empirical study conducted for this book, I replicate and extend several findings by Zacher and Baumeister (2024) by investigating expanded sets of individual and work characteristics, as well as important work and life outcomes, in relation to the three dimensions of the good working life.

Finally, Zacher and Baumeister (2024) explored the job titles reported by participants in their initial study. They presented selected examples of job titles of workers scoring both very high (i.e., one standard deviation above the mean) or very low (i.e., one standard deviation below the mean) on each dimension of the good working life, after correcting for the respective other two dimensions. As shown in Table 2.2, which is taken from Zacher and Baumeister (2024), example job titles of workers who reported high job satisfaction include architects, human resources officers, and software developers, whereas dental assistants, plant operators, and secretaries reported relatively low levels of job satisfaction. The examples of job titles of workers who scored high on work meaningfulness included teachers, nurses, and firefighters, whereas insurance employees, translators, and travel agents scored low on work meaningfulness. The examples of job titles of people who report having a psychologically rich working life include prison guards, flight attendants, special education workers, and art dealers, whereas librarians, accountants, and janitors scored low on this dimension. Generally, these findings seem to suggest that more intellectually challenging professional jobs are associated with higher job satisfaction scores, whereas jobs related to social services and safety tend to be associated with higher work meaningfulness scores. Finally, jobs related to

Table 2.2 Illustrative examples of jobs titles (from Zacher & Baumeister, 2024)

Dimension of the good working life	*Low scoring jobs*	*High scoring jobs*
Job satisfaction	• Dental assistant • Warehouse shipping packer • Plant operator • Postal carrier • Secretary	• Architect • Human resources officer • Project manager • Software developer • Tax consultant
Work meaningfulness	• Business-to-business sales consultant • Insurance employee • Translator • Travel agent • Web designer	• Educator • Firefighter • Physician, nurse • Teacher • Medical assistant
Work psychological richness	• Accountant • Cleaning staff • Janitor • Librarian • Packer	• Lawyer • Prison guard • Flight or train attendant • Immigrant assistance • Special education worker • Art dealer

higher work psychological richness scores seemed to involve more interesting and complex tasks, as well as the potential for varied positive and negative work experiences. In Chap. 5, I extend these initial results by analyzing workers' scores on the three good working life dimensions across 21 different industries represented in the new study conducted for this book.

What Kind of Working Life Do People Want?

Oishi and colleagues asked study participants from nine different countries what kind of life they would choose if they could only choose one out of three possible lives for themselves—a happy life, a meaningful life, or a psychologically rich life. Their findings showed that most participants (approximately 50% or more) prioritized a happy life, followed by a meaningful life (between 19% and 39% across countries) and a psychologically rich life (between 7% and 17%; Oishi & Westgate, 2022). More specifically, the descriptive statistics for participants in Germany were 49.7% for a happy life, 33.5% for a meaningful life, and 16.8% for a psychologically rich life. Interestingly, the German respondents reported higher preferences for a psychologically rich life than respondents from the other eight countries, including the United States, Norway, Portugal, Japan, Korea, Singapore, India, and Angola.

In the empirical study conducted for this book, I asked the same question as Oishi and colleagues to the employed participants in the Time 2 survey (see left part of Fig. 2.1). Of the 1342 respondents, approximately 52% indicated that they would choose the satisfied and happy life, replicating the findings of Oishi and Westgate (2022). Interestingly, however, only approximately 21% indicated that they would choose the meaningful and fulfilling life, and 27% indicated that they would choose the eventful and interesting, psychologically rich life. Thus, compared to Oishi and colleagues' study, more participants in the study conducted for this book prioritized the psychologically rich life, while relatively fewer participants chose the meaningful life. A possible reason for these differences across studies may be that all participants in the study conducted for this book were in paid employment, whereas Oishi and colleagues relied mostly on samples of college students and paid online survey takers (Oishi et al., 2020).

In the empirical study conducted for this book, I also asked the employed participants which working life they would choose if they could only choose one out of three possible options: a satisfied working life, a meaningful working life, or a psychologically rich working life (see right part of Fig. 2.1). Of the 1353 respondents, approximately 48% indicated

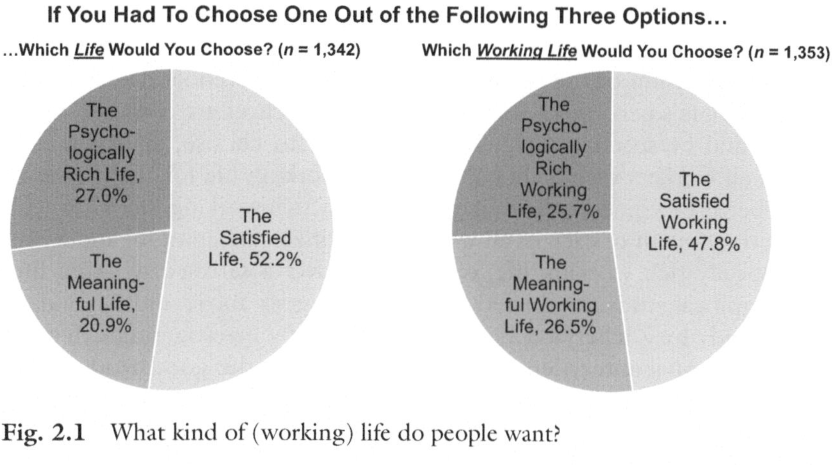

Fig. 2.1 What kind of (working) life do people want?

that they would choose the satisfied and happy working life, whereas approximately 26% each indicated that they would choose a meaningful working life or a psychologically rich working life, respectively. Thus, similar to life in general, the satisfied working life was also the most popular, but the alternative options of a meaningful and a psychologically rich working life were also frequently chosen, with about one-fourth of workers opting for each of these two options.

Generally, most workers would probably like to experience high levels in all three dimensions of a good working life, including high job satisfaction, high work meaningfulness, and high work psychological richness. However, the results of the survey study conducted for this book suggest that workers differ with regard to which of the three dimensions is most important to them personally. It is remarkable that approximately one-fourth of the workers surveyed said that a meaningful and fulfilling working life is most desirable to them, and another one-fourth of the workers prioritized an eventful and interesting working life over a working life that is characterized by high levels of job satisfaction. These findings also provide evidence for the usefulness of the tripartite conceptualization of the good working life.

Summary

The good working life involves a combination of high levels of job satisfaction, work meaningfulness, and work psychological richness. Whereas job satisfaction is characterized by a positive and pleasurable work-related state, work meaningfulness relates to people's sense that their work is important and contributes to their personal growth and purpose. The newest dimension of the good working life, work psychological richness, entails people's perception that their work experiences are complex, interesting, and perspective-changing. If they had to choose, approximately half of all workers would choose a satisfied working life for themselves at the expense of a meaningful or psychologically rich working life. However, about one-fourth of each of all workers prioritize a meaningful and a psychologically rich working life, respectively, over a satisfied working life. The empirical study conducted for this book goes above and beyond an initial study by Zacher and Baumeister (2024) by investigating extended sets of potential antecedents and consequences of the good working life among a large sample of workers from different jobs, organizations, and industries. The measures and analyses used in this new empirical study are described in the next chapter.

References

Allan, B. A., Batz-Barbarich, C., Sterling, H. M., & Tay, L. (2019). Outcomes of meaningful work: A meta-analysis. *Journal of Management Studies, 56*(3), 500–528. https://doi.org/10.1111/joms.12406

Barrick, M. R., Mount, M. K., & Li, N. (2013). The theory of purposeful work behavior: The role of personality, job characteristics, and experienced meaningfulness. *Academy of Management Review, 38*(1), 132–153. https://doi.org/10.5465/amr.2010.0479

Baumeister, R. F., Vohs, K. D., Aaker, J. L., & Garbinsky, E. N. (2013). Some key differences between a happy life and a meaningful life. *Journal of Positive Psychology, 8*(6), 505–516. https://doi.org/10.1080/17439760.2013.830764

Besser, L. L., & Oishi, S. (2020). The psychologically rich life. *Philosophical Psychology, 33*(8), 1053–1071. https://doi.org/10.1080/09515089.2020.1778662

Blustein, D. L., Lysova, E. I., & Duffy, R. D. (2023). Understanding decent work and meaningful work. *Annual Review of Organizational Psychology and Organizational Behavior, 10*, 289–314. https://doi.org/10.1146/annurev-orgpsych-031921-024847

Bunderson, J. S., & Thompson, J. A. (2009). The call of the wild: Zookeepers, callings, and the double-edged sword of deeply meaningful work. *Administrative Science Quarterly, 54*, 32–57. https://doi.org/10.2189/asqu.2009.54.1.32

Duffy, R. D., Autin, K. L., & Bott, E. M. (2015). Work volition and job satisfaction: Examining the role of work meaning and person–environment fit. *The Career Development Quarterly, 63*(2), 126–140. https://doi.org/10.1002/cdq.12009

Harrison, D. A., Newman, D. A., & Roth, P. L. (2006). How important are job attitudes? Meta-analytic comparisons of integrative behavioral outcomes and time sequences. *Academy of Management Journal, 49*(2), 305–325. https://doi.org/10.5465/AMJ.2006.20786077

Judge, T. A., & Kammeyer-Mueller, J. D. (2012). Job attitudes. *Annual Review of Psychology, 63*, 341–367. https://doi.org/10.1146/annurev-psych-120710-100511

Judge, T. A., & Klinger, R. (2008). Job satisfaction: Subjective well-being at work. In M. Eid & R. J. Larsen (Eds.), *The science of subjective well-being* (pp. 393–413). Guilford Press.

Judge, T. A., Weiss, H. M., Kammeyer-Mueller, J. D., & Hulin, C. L. (2017). Job attitudes, job satisfaction, and job affect: A century of continuity and of change. *Journal of Applied Psychology, 102*(3), 356–374. https://doi.org/10.1037/apl0000181

Locke, E. A. (1976). The nature and causes of job satisfaction. In M. D. Dunnette (Ed.), *Handbook of industrial and organizational psychology* (pp. 1297–1349). Rand McNally.

Oishi, S., Choi, H., Koo, M., Galinha, I., Ishii, K., Komiya, A., et al. (2020). Happiness, meaning, and psychological richness. *Affective Science, 1*, 107–115. https://doi.org/10.1007/s42761-020-00011-z

Oishi, S., Choi, H., Liu, A., & Kurtz, J. (2021). Experiences associated with psychological richness. *European Journal of Personality, 35*(5), 754–770. https://doi.org/10.1177/0890207020962334

Oishi, S., & Westgate, E. C. (2022). A psychologically rich life: Beyond happiness and meaning. *Psychological Review, 129*(4), 790–811. https://doi.org/10.1037/rev0000317

Rosso, B. D., Dekas, K. H., & Wrzesniewski, A. (2010). On the meaning of work: A theoretical integration and review. *Research in Organizational Behavior, 30*, 91–127. https://doi.org/10.1016/j.riob.2010.09.001

Ryan, R. M., & Deci, E. L. (2001). On happiness and human potentials: A review of research on hedonic and eudaimonic well-being. *Annual Review of Psychology, 52*(1), 141–166. https://doi.org/10.1146/annurev.psych.52.1.141

Schmitt, A., Zacher, H., & Frese, M. (2012). The buffering effect of selection, optimization, and compensation strategy use on the relationship between problem solving demands and occupational well-being: A daily diary study. *Journal of Occupational Health Psychology, 17*, 139–149. https://doi.org/10.1037/a0027054

Sonnentag, S. (2015). Dynamics of well-being. *Annual Review of Organizational Psychology and Organizational Behavior, 2*, 261–293. https://doi.org/10.1146/annurev-orgpsych-032414-111347

Steger, M. F., Dik, B. J., & Duffy, R. D. (2012). Measuring meaningful work: The work and meaning inventory (WAMI). *Journal of Career Assessment, 20*(3), 322–337. https://doi.org/10.1177/1069072711436160

Weiss, H. M., & Cropanzano, R. (1996). Affective Events Theory: A theoretical discussion of the structure, causes and consequences of affective experiences at work. In B. M. Staw & L. L. Cummings (Eds.), *Research in Organizational Behavior* (pp. 1–74). JAI Press.

Zacher, H., & Baumeister, R. F. (2024). Differences among a satisfied, a meaningful, and a psychologically rich working life. *Journal of Positive Psychology.* https://doi.org/10.1080/17439760.2024.2417102

CHAPTER 3

Measuring and Analyzing the Good Working Life

Abstract In this chapter, I describe how the three dimensions of the good working life—job satisfaction, work meaningfulness, and work psychological richness—were operationalized in the empirical study conducted for this book. I report example items and reliabilities for each survey questionnaire, as well as bivariate correlations among the three measures of the good working life. Additionally, I describe several alternative measures to operationalize the three dimensions of the good working life. I further describe the analytical approach—partial correlation analyses—used in the subsequent chapters of this book. The three dimensions of the good working life were assessed reliably and, despite relatively strong intercorrelations, represented distinct constructs.

Keywords Measurement • Methodology • Survey study • Analyses • Statistics • Partial correlations

The good working life is not a unidimensional concept but consists of three distinct dimensions: job satisfaction, work meaningfulness, and work psychological richness. Accordingly, multiple measurement instruments are needed to operationalize the good working life. There are several instruments available in the psychological literature to assess each of the three dimensions of the good working life. In this chapter, I outline how

H. Zacher, *The Good Working Life*,
https://doi.org/10.1007/978-3-031-77221-4_3

I measured job satisfaction, work meaningfulness, and work psychological richness using self-report questionnaires in the empirical study conducted for this book. Example items, response formats, and sources for each measure of the good working life are shown in Table 3.1. The original sources cited in the table include the full measures (i.e., all items). Additionally, where available, I describe alternative measures for the three dimensions of the good working life. Toward the end of the chapter, I describe the approach I used to analyze the data collected in the study conducted for this book (i.e., partial correlation analyses).

Table 3.1 Example items from scales used to measure the good working life

Dimension	*Example items*	*Source*
Job satisfaction	(1) "I feel fairly well satisfied with my present job." (2) "Most days I am enthusiastic about my work." (3) "I find real enjoyment in my work." Response format: 7-point Likert scale from 1 = *strongly disagree* to 7 = *strongly agree*	Judge et al. (1998)
Work meaningfulness	(1) "I have a good sense of what makes my job meaningful." (Subdimension: personal meaning in work) (2) "I view my work as contributing to my personal growth." (Subdimension: meaning making through work) (3) "I know my work makes a positive difference in the world." (Subdimension: greater good motivations) Response format: 7-point Likert scale from 1 = *strongly disagree* to 7 = *strongly agree*	Steger et al. (2012)
Work psychological richness	(1) "I have a lot of interesting experiences at my work." (2) "My working life consists of rich, intense moments." (3) "I have a lot of stories about my work to tell others." Response format: 7-point Likert scale from 1 = *strongly disagree* to 7 = *strongly agree*	Zacher and Baumeister (2024), adapted from Oishi et al. (2019)

Measuring Job Satisfaction

In both the empirical study conducted for this book and the initial study on the good working life published in the *Journal of Positive Psychology* (Zacher & Baumeister, 2024), I assessed job satisfaction with a widely used five-item self-report questionnaire (Judge et al., 1998). The items included in this scale operationalize job satisfaction consistent with its definition as a positive and pleasurable emotional state that results from people's evaluations of their jobs and job-related experiences (Locke, 1976). An example item is "I feel fairly well satisfied with my present job," and the response options range from 1 = *strongly disagree* to 7 = *strongly agree* on a 7-point Likert scale. Of note, two items included in this measure are negatively worded and need to be reverse coded before averaging the scores to create a composite score for each participant. Given certain methodological problems associated with the practice of reversed items (see Weijters et al., 2013), it may be an option to use only the three positively worded items, especially when participant time is limited in large-scale panel studies. Additionally, there are several alternative multi-item job satisfaction measures available in the literature (see Van Saane et al., 2003, for a review). Finally, it is also very common to measure job satisfaction with a reliable, valid, and practical single-item measure: "All things considered, how satisfied are you with your job in general?" (Dolbier et al., 2005; Wanous et al., 1997).

Measuring Work Meaningfulness

In the empirical study conducted for this book, I measured work meaningfulness with the ten items from the work and meaning inventory (WAMI) developed and validated by Steger et al. (2012). Based on a multidimensional model of work as subjectively meaningful, these researchers developed items to assess people's experience of personal meaning in work, meaning making through work, and greater good motivations (see Chap. 2 for definitions of these facets of work meaningfulness). Example items are "I have a good sense of what makes my job meaningful" (personal meaning in work), "I view my work as contributing to my personal growth" (meaning making through work), and "I know my work makes a positive difference in the world" (greater good motivations). Participants' responses are recorded on a 7-point Likert scale ranging from 1 = *strongly disagree* to 7 = *strongly agree*. Scores on the ten items are averaged to create an overall work meaningfulness score for each participant (none of the items need to be reverse coded). The goal of the empirical study conducted for this book was to obtain a comprehensive measure of workers' experiences of work meaningfulness. In future studies, depending on their focus, researchers could also opt to include only one or two of the three subdimensions of work meaningfulness.

In the initial study on the good working life (Zacher & Baumeister, 2024), work meaningfulness was measured with a reliable and validated 5-item scale that focuses on the greater good motivations subdimension of work meaningfulness, that is, people's experience that their work contributes in important ways to other people and society in general (Bunderson & Thompson, 2009). Example items from that scale are "The work that I do is important," "The work that I do makes the world a better place," and "What I do at work makes a difference in the world." Finally, a few additional measures of work meaningfulness exist in the literature (see Arnold et al., 2007; Hackman & Oldham, 1976; May et al., 2004; Spreitzer, 1995).

Measuring Work Psychological Richness

As in the study by Zacher and Baumeister (2024), I measured work psychological richness in the empirical study conducted for this book with a 12-item scale adapted from the short version of the psychological richness questionnaire developed and validated by Oishi et al. (2019). I adapted each of the 12 items to refer to the work context in the present tense. The original items of the psychological richness questionnaire are worded in the present perfect tense and focus on life in general, not on the work context. Example items of the adapted measure are "I have a lot of interesting experiences at my work," "My working life consists of rich, intense moments," and "I have a lot of stories about my work to tell others." The response format was also a 7-point Likert scale ranging from 1 = *strongly disagree* to 7 = *strongly agree*. In their scale validation article, Oishi et al. (2019) also reported 19-item and 36-item versions of the psychological richness questionnaire that could be used in future research. So far, apart from Oishi et al. (2019) and the adapted version of Zacher and Baumeister (2024), no other measures of psychological richness and work psychological richness, respectively, exist in the literature.

Correlations Among the Dimensions of the Good Working Life

Figure 3.1 shows one example item per dimension, means and standard deviations, Cronbach's alpha reliabilities (scores of 0.70 and greater are generally considered acceptable), and correlations between the three measures collected in the empirical study conducted for this book. Means represent the average scores across participants on each questionnaire, and standard deviations represent measures of the amount of variation of the scores of a construct across participants. For 7-point scales, standard deviations of approximately 1.0 are typical and may indicate a normal, bell-shaped distribution of the scores.

As shown in Fig. 3.1, participants on average reported scores that were somewhat higher than the mid-points of the 7-point scales (i.e., higher than 4) and demonstrated quite a bit of variability. Specifically, the mean

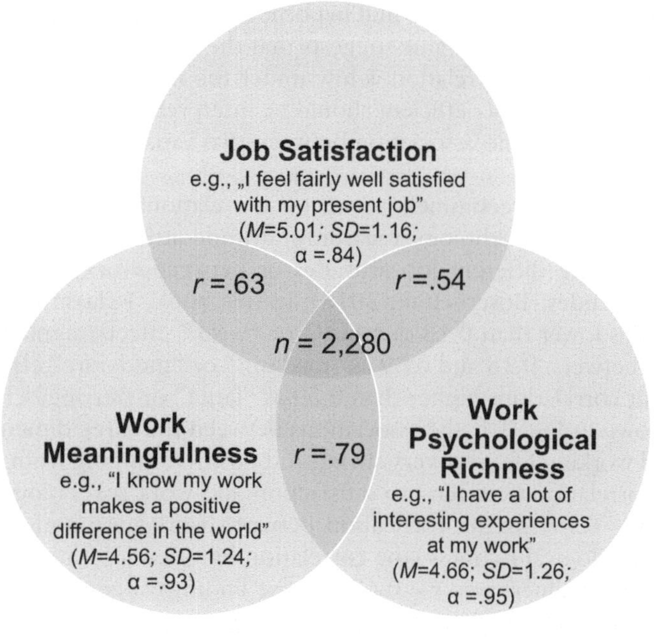

Fig. 3.1 Example items, reliabilities, and correlations between measures of the good working life

for job satisfaction was 5.01 on a 7-point scale (standard deviation = 1.16), the mean for work meaningfulness was 4.56 on a 7-point scale (standard deviation = 1.24), and the mean for work psychological richness was 4.66 on a 7-point scale (standard deviation = 1.26). Moreover, the reliabilities in the current study were all higher than 0.80 and, for work meaningfulness and work psychological richness, even higher than 0.90. These findings suggest that job satisfaction, work meaningfulness, and work psychological richness were measured in a reliable and consistent way in this study.

A correlation coefficient represents an estimate of the strength and direction of an association between two measures. Correlation coefficients can range from $r = -1.0$ (a perfect negative relation) to $r = +1.0$ (a perfect positive relation). A correlation of $r = 0$ indicates the absence of a relation between two variables. When positive or negative correlations are "statistically significant," that is, go along with a p-value below 0.05, this means that the probability of obtaining a correlation of at least the same size as actually observed under the assumption that the relation does *not* exist (i.e., the assumption that the "null hypothesis" is correct) is relatively low. In other words, a small p-value suggests that the likelihood of an observed positive or negative correlation is low under the null hypothesis. A non-significant correlation coefficient should be interpreted as not distinguishable from zero (i.e., no association between two variables can be assumed based on the data).

Consistent with recommendations for correlational effect size benchmarks in applied psychology regarding attitude-attitude relations (e.g., relations among different job attitudes or between work characteristics and job attitudes; Bosco et al., 2015), in this book, I classify significant correlations lower than 0.18 as "small" or "weak" effects, significant correlations between 0.18 and 0.39 as "medium" or "moderate" effects, and significant correlations higher than 0.39 as "large" or "strong" effects.

As shown in Fig. 3.1, the associations between the three dimensions of the good working life were very strong and positive, ranging from $r = 0.53$ for the correlation between job satisfaction and work psychological richness to $r = 0.79$ for the correlation between work meaningfulness and work psychological richness (the correlation between job satisfaction and work meaningfulness was $r = 0.63$). These findings suggest that workers who are more satisfied with their jobs also tend to perceive their work as more meaningful and as more psychologically rich, and vice versa. In contrast, workers who are less satisfied with their jobs also tend to perceive their work as less meaningful and as less psychologically rich, and vice versa. However, the fact that the correlations were far from perfect (i.e., $r = 1.0$) suggests that the constructs measure different aspects of the good working life.

Analytical Approach

The primary goal of the empirical study conducted for this book was to obtain an understanding of the *unique* relations between the three dimensions of the good working life and other variables, including individual and work characteristics, as well as work and life outcomes. As the three dimensions of the good working life are strongly correlated, it is necessary to "partial out" the effects of the other two dimensions of the good working life in order to obtain estimates of the unique relationships between one dimension of the good working life and other variables. Accordingly, the primary analytical strategy I adopted in this book, consistent with Baumeister et al. (2013) and Zacher and Baumeister (2024), was to compute *partial correlations* between each of the three dimensions of the good working life and other variables, always controlling for the respective other two dimensions of the good working life (when other analytical approaches are used, such as regression analyses in Chap. 4 to examine effects of the use of character strengths, this will be explained in the respective chapter).

A partial correlation is a measure of the strength and direction of a linear relationship between two variables (e.g., age and job satisfaction) while accounting for the effects of other variables. These other variables are called covariates or control variables and are, in this case, the respective other two dimensions of the good working life (e.g., work meaningfulness and work psychological richness when the focal association involves job satisfaction). This analytical approach corresponds to running several regression analyses (see Cohen et al., 2013) in which the three dimensions of the good working life are entered simultaneously as predictors of each individual or work characteristic or each work or life outcome. Thus, each partial correlation represents an estimate of the unique association between one of the dimensions of the good working life and another construct that is statistically independent of the other two dimensions of the good working life.

Summary

The three dimensions of the good working life—job satisfaction, work meaningfulness, and work psychological richness—can be measured in a reliable and valid way using relatively short self-report questionnaires. In the empirical study conducted for this book, participants provided a broad range of responses on each of the three measures, with average scores slightly higher than the mid-points of the respective scales. Different alternative measures, including both multi-item scales and single items, exist for job satisfaction and work meaningfulness, whereas so far, only one questionnaire (albeit in multiple versions with different numbers of items) exists for the relatively novel construct of work psychological richness. The three dimensions of the good working life are strongly and positively correlated but represent distinct constructs.

References

Arnold, K. A., Turner, N., Barling, J., Kelloway, E. K., & McKee, M. C. (2007). Transformational leadership and psychological well-being: The mediating role of meaningful work. *Journal of Occupational Health Psychology, 12*(3), 193–203. https://doi.org/10.1037/1076-8998.12.3.193

Baumeister, R. F., Vohs, K. D., Aaker, J. L., & Garbinsky, E. N. (2013). Some key differences between a happy life and a meaningful life. *Journal of Positive Psychology, 8*(6), 505–516. https://doi.org/10.1080/17439760.2013.830764

Bosco, F. A., Aguinis, H., Singh, K., Field, J. G., & Pierce, C. A. (2015). Correlational effect size benchmarks. *Journal of Applied Psychology, 100*, 431–449. https://doi.org/10.1037/a0038047

Bunderson, J. S., & Thompson, J. A. (2009). The call of the wild: Zookeepers, callings, and the double-edged sword of deeply meaningful work. *Administrative Science Quarterly, 54*, 32–57. https://doi.org/10.2189/asqu.2009.54.1.32

Cohen, J., Cohen, P., West, S. G., & Aiken, L. S. (2013). *Applied multiple regression/correlation analysis for the behavioral sciences.* Routledge.

Dolbier, C. L., Webster, J. A., McCalister, K. T., Mallon, M. W., & Steinhardt, M. A. (2005). Reliability and validity of a single-item measure of job satisfaction. *American Journal of Health Promotion, 19*(3), 194–198. https://doi.org/10.4278/0890-1171-19.3.194

Hackman, J. R., & Oldham, G. R. (1976). Motivation through the design of work: Test of a theory. *Organizational Behavior and Human Performance, 16*, 250–279. https://doi.org/10.1016/0030-5073(76)90016-7

Judge, T. A., Locke, E. A., Durham, C. C., & Kluger, A. N. (1998). Dispositional effects on job and life satisfaction: The role of core evaluations. *Journal of Applied Psychology, 83*(1), 17–34. https://doi.org/10.1037/0021-9010.83.1.17

Locke, E. A. (1976). The nature and causes of job satisfaction. In M. D. Dunnette (Ed.), *Handbook of industrial and organizational psychology* (pp. 1297–1349). Rand McNally.

May, D. R., Gilson, R. L., & Harter, L. M. (2004). The psychological conditions of meaningfulness, safety and availability and the engagement of the human spirit at work. *Journal of Occupational and Organizational Psychology, 77*, 11–37. https://doi.org/10.1348/096317904322915892

Oishi, S., Choi, H., Buttrick, N., Heintzelman, S. J., Kushlev, K., Westgate, E. C., et al. (2019). The psychologically rich life questionnaire. *Journal of Research in Personality, 81*, 257–270. https://doi.org/10.1016/j.jrp.2019.06.010

Spreitzer, G. M. (1995). Psychological empowerment in the workplace: Dimensions, measurement, and validation. *Academy of Management Journal, 38*(5), 1442–1465. https://doi.org/10.5465/256865

Steger, M. F., Dik, B. J., & Duffy, R. D. (2012). Measuring meaningful work: The work and meaning inventory (WAMI). *Journal of Career Assessment, 20*(3), 322–337. https://doi.org/10.1177/1069072711436160

Van Saane, N., Sluiter, J. K., Verbeek, J. H. A. M., & Frings-Dresen, M. H. (2003). Reliability and validity of instruments measuring job satisfaction – A systematic review. *Occupational Medicine, 53*(3), 191–200. https://doi.org/10.1093/occmed/kqg038

Wanous, J. P., Reichers, A. E., & Hudy, M. J. (1997). Overall job satisfaction: How good are single-item measures? *Journal of Applied Psychology, 82*(2), 247–252. https://doi.org/10.1037/0021-9010.82.2.247

Weijters, B., Baumgartner, H., & Schillewaert, N. (2013). Reversed item bias: An integrative model. *Psychological Methods, 18*(3), 320–334. https://doi.org/10.1037/a0032121

Zacher, H., & Baumeister, R. F. (2024). Differences among a satisfied, a meaningful, and a psychologically rich working life. *Journal of Positive Psychology*. https://doi.org/10.1080/17439760.2024.2417102

CHAPTER 4

Individual Characteristics and the Good Working Life

Abstract This chapter focuses on the unique relations between the three dimensions of the good working life—job satisfaction, work meaningfulness, and work psychological richness—and various individual difference characteristics. These characteristics include demographic characteristics (e.g., age, sex), personality characteristics (e.g., Big Five characteristics, dark triad traits), the use of character strengths at work, and job crafting behaviors. Results of the empirical study conducted for this book showed that job satisfaction had the strongest partial correlations with core self-evaluations, emotional stability, and conscientiousness. The strongest partial correlations for work meaningfulness were with proactive personality, as well as task and cognitive job crafting. Finally, work psychological richness had the strongest partial correlations with extraversion, openness to experience, and proactive personality.

Keywords Individual differences • Demographic characteristics • Personality • Big Five • Core self-evaluations • Psychological capital • Proactive personality • Character strengths • Job crafting

Who is more likely and who is less likely to experience a good working life? The goal of this chapter is to examine the unique relations between various individual characteristics (including demographic characteristics,

H. Zacher, *The Good Working Life*,
https://doi.org/10.1007/978-3-031-77221-4_4

personality characteristics, use of character strengths at work, and job crafting behaviors) and job satisfaction, work meaningfulness, and work psychological richness. Table 4.1 provides an overview of the demographic and personality characteristics that were considered as potential antecedents of the good working life in the study conducted for this book, including definitions, example items, response formats, reliability estimates, and sources of the measures.

Demographic Characteristics

The demographic characteristics included in the empirical study conducted for this book were age, sex, education, nationality, and migration background. Note that, unlike in the United States, "race/ethnicity" is traditionally not assessed in studies with samples from Germany. I did not have *a priori* expectations regarding relations between demographic characteristics and the three dimensions of the good working life, with the exception of the relations between age and job satisfaction and work meaningfulness. Consistent with propositions of the lifespan developmental theory of socioemotional selectivity (Carstensen et al., 1999), a meta-analysis on age and job attitudes reported a positive association between age and job satisfaction (Ng & Feldman, 2010). According to socioemotional selectivity theory, older workers perceive their remaining future time as more limited than younger workers and, therefore, are more likely to prioritize positive emotions and meaningful experiences at work (Rudolph et al., 2018; Zacher & Frese, 2009). I therefore expected that worker age would be positively associated with job satisfaction and work meaningfulness in the study.

The results of the partial correlation analyses for the demographic and personality characteristics are summarized in Table 4.2. Consistent with expectations, older workers reported slightly higher job satisfaction than younger workers. Unexpectedly, however, there was a weak negative association between age and work meaningfulness and a weak positive association between age and work psychological richness. These findings suggest that older workers experienced slightly lower work meaningfulness and slightly higher work psychological richness, compared to younger workers. The partial correlations between the other demographic characteristics and the three dimensions of the good working life were also relatively small or not significant. While there was no significant sex difference in job satisfaction, women reported slightly lower work meaningfulness and

Table 4.1 Demographic and personality characteristics: definitions and operationalizations

Construct	*Definition*	*Example item (number of items in parentheses, unless single item)*	*Response format*	*Cronbach's alpha reliability*	*Source*
Demographic characteristics					
Age	Chronological age (time lived since birth)	"Please indicate your age in years."	Open answer	–	Schwall (2012)
Sex	Biological sex	"Please indicate your sex."	Three options: 1 = male, 2 = female, 3 = diverse (the third option was excluded in the analyses due to small number of participants in this category [$n = 2$])	–	–
Education	Highest level of education achieved	"What is your highest educational degree?"	Five options: 1 = no degree, 2 = lower secondary school degree, 3 = intermediate secondary school degree, 4 = upper secondary school degree, 5 = technical college/college/university degree	–	–
Nationality	Status of belonging to a particular country	"Please indicate your nationality."	Two options: 1 = Germany, 2 = other country	–	–

(continued)

Table 4.1 (continued)

Construct	*Definition*	*Example item (number of items in parentheses, unless single item)*	*Response format*	*Cronbach's alpha reliability*	*Source*
Migration background	Oneself or at least one parent was born in a different country than Germany	"Do you have a migration background, that is, do you or at least one of your parents not have German citizenship from birth?"	Two options: 1 = no, 2 = yes	–	–
Personality characteristics					
Extraversion	Tendency to be outgoing/energetic versus solitary/reserved	"I see myself as someone who is outgoing, sociable." (4)	7-point Likert scale ranging from 1 = *strongly disagree* to 7 = *strongly agree*	0.78	Rammstedt and John (2005)
Agreeableness	Tendency to be friendly/compassionate versus critical/judgmental	"I see myself as someone who is generally trusting." (4)	7-point Likert scale ranging from 1 = *strongly disagree* to 7 = *strongly agree*	0.64	Rammstedt and John (2005)
Conscientiousness	Tendency to be efficient/organized versus extravagant/careless	"I see myself as someone who does a thorough job." (4)	7-point Likert scale ranging from 1 = *strongly disagree* to 7 = *strongly agree*	0.76	Rammstedt and John (2005)
Emotional stability	Tendency to be resilient/confident versus sensitive/nervous	"I see myself as someone who is relaxed, handles stress well." (4)	7-point Likert scale ranging from 1 = *strongly disagree* to 7 = *strongly agree*	0.81	Rammstedt and John (2005)
Openness to experience	Tendency to be inventive/curious versus consistent/cautious	"I see myself as someone who has an active imagination." (5)	7-point Likert scale ranging from 1 = *strongly disagree* to 7 = *strongly agree*	0.75	Rammstedt and John (2005)

Core self-evaluations	Higher-order construct that integrates generalized self-efficacy, self-esteem, emotional stability, and internal locus of control	"I am confident I get the success I deserve in life." (generalized self-efficacy), "Overall, I am satisfied with myself." (self-esteem), "I am capable of coping with most of my problems." (emotional stability), "I determine what will happen in my life." (internal locus of control) (12)	7-point Likert scale ranging from 1 = *strongly disagree* to 7 = *strongly agree*	0.88	Judge et al. (2003)
Psychological capital	Higher-order construct that integrates hope, efficacy, resilience, and optimism	"If I should find myself in a jam, I could think of many ways to get out of it." (hope), "I am confident that I could deal efficiently with unexpected events." (efficacy), "I consider myself to be able to stand a lot, I am not easily discouraged by failure." (resilience), "I am looking forward to the life ahead of me." (optimism) (12)	7-point Likert scale ranging from 1 = *strongly disagree* to 7 = *strongly agree*	0.94	Lorenz et al. (2022)

(*continued*)

Table 4.1 (continued)

Construct	*Definition*	*Example item (number of items in parentheses, unless single item)*	*Response format*	*Cronbach's alpha reliability*	*Source*
Proactive personality	Tendency to take personal initiative and to initiate change	"If I see something I don't like, I fix it." (10)	7-point Likert scale ranging from 1 = *strongly disagree* to 7 = *strongly agree*	0.92	Seibert et al. (1999)
Machiavellianism	Tendency to manipulate and exploit others	"I have used deceit or lied to get my way." (4)	7-point Likert scale ranging from 1 = *strongly disagree* to 7 = *strongly agree*	0.92	Jonason and Webster (2010); Küfner et al. (2014)
Psychopathy	Tendency to show antisocial behavior, impulsivity, thrill seeking, and callousness	"I tend to lack remorse." (4)	7-point Likert scale ranging from 1 = *strongly disagree* to 7 = *strongly agree*	0.82	Jonason and Webster (2010); Küfner et al. (2014)
Narcissism	Tendency to demonstrate grandiosity, entitlement, dominance, and superiority	"I tend to want others to admire me." (4)	7-point Likert scale ranging from 1 = *strongly disagree* to 7 = *strongly agree*	0.89	Jonason and Webster (2010); Küfner et al. (2014)

Table 4.2 Partial correlations between demographic and personality characteristics and dimensions of the good working life (corrected for the respective other two dimensions of the good working life)

	Job satisfaction	*Work meaningfulness*	*Work psychological richness*
Demographic characteristics			
Age	0.09	−0.08	0.07
Sex (1 = male, 2 = female)	(−0.01)	−0.06	0.06
Education	−0.07	0.09	(0.01)
Nationality (1 = German citizen, 2 = other citizenship)	(−0.02)	(0.04)	−0.07
Migration background (1 = no, 2 = yes)	(−0.02)	(−0.01)	(−0.01)
Personality characteristics			
Extraversion	0.09	(0.001)	0.16
Agreeableness	0.11	0.14	−0.08
Conscientiousness	0.20	(0.04)	0.09
Emotional stability	0.30	(0.02)	(0.02)
Openness to experience	(−0.01)	0.09	0.16
Core self-evaluations	0.36	0.05	0.06
Psychological capital[a]	0.16	0.14	0.15
Proactive personality	(−0.03)	0.18	0.20
Machiavellianism	−0.20	(−0.01)	0.09
Psychopathy	−0.19	(−0.04)	0.08
Narcissism	−0.18	0.12	0.05

Note: N = Due to missing data, N ranged from 1906 to 2048

[a] N = 1325–1328 (assessed at Time 2). Non-significant correlations ($p > 0.05$) are shown in parentheses

slightly higher work psychological richness than men. In terms of education, workers with a higher educational degree reported slightly lower job satisfaction and slightly higher work meaningfulness than workers with a lower educational degree, whereas there was no significant association for work psychological richness. Foreigners reported slightly lower work psychological richness than German citizens, whereas there were no significant nationality differences regarding job satisfaction and work meaningfulness. Finally, there were also no significant differences in the three dimensions of the good working life depending on whether participants had a migration background or not. Overall, these findings suggest that demographic characteristics do not play a major role for the good working life, but future research could still consider age, sex, and educational level as potential control variables, especially when the sample composition is very heterogeneous.

Big Five Personality Characteristics

In the empirical study conducted for this book, personality was conceptualized and measured in terms of several different constructs that are well-established in the psychological literature. It is likely that personality characteristics are associated with job satisfaction because job satisfaction is a cognitive-affective (i.e., attitudinal) reaction to people's perceptions of their job, work-related experiences, and the work environment, which are influenced by their personal dispositions (Judge & Kammeyer-Mueller, 2012). Moreover, according to the theory of purposeful work behavior (Barrick et al., 2013), certain personality traits may activate workers' striving toward personal goals in the work context and, thus, lead to experiencing greater work meaningfulness. Finally, research on personality characteristics and psychological richness in general is so far limited (Oishi & Westgate, 2022), but it seems likely that experiencing work as characterized by complexity, a variety of interesting and perspective-changing experiences, and a variety of deep emotions is also linked to certain dispositional tendencies.

The Big Five characteristics include extraversion (i.e., the dispositional tendency to be outgoing/energetic vs. solitary/reserved), agreeableness (friendly/compassionate vs. critical/judgmental), conscientiousness (efficient/organized vs. extravagant/careless), emotional stability (resilient/confident vs. sensitive/nervous), and openness to experience (inventive/curious vs. consistent/cautious) (Digman, 1990; McCrae & Costa, 1997). The Big Five personality characteristics reflect the "bright side" of personality, as high levels of these traits (especially emotional stability, conscientiousness, and agreeableness) are associated with personal maturity, adjustment, as well as emotional intelligence (McCrae & Costa, 1997; Staudinger & Kunzmann, 2005; Van der Linden et al., 2017). Furthermore, developmental psychologists have argued that openness to experience reflects personal growth (Staudinger & Kunzmann, 2005).

Several studies have examined associations between the Big Five personality characteristics and job satisfaction. A meta-analysis based on 163 independent samples reported moderate and positive average associations (corrected for statistical artifacts, such as sample size and measurement unreliability) between job satisfaction and extraversion ($\rho = 0.25$), agreeableness ($\rho = 0.17$), conscientiousness ($\rho = 0.26$), and emotional stability ($\rho = 0.29$), but only a weak relation with openness to experience ($\rho = 0.02$; Judge et al., 2002). These findings suggest that people who tend to experience more positive (i.e., extraversion) and fewer negative emotions (i.e., emotional stability) and that people who tend to get along with others (i.e., agreeableness) and are dependable and achievement-oriented (i.e., conscientiousness) are more likely to experience higher job satisfaction. However, previous studies on the Big Five personality characteristics and job satisfaction did not control for the other two dimensions of the good working life. Nevertheless, I expected that job satisfaction would be positively related to extraversion, agreeableness, conscientiousness, and emotional stability. In contrast, I did not expect a strong association between job satisfaction and openness to experience.

Results of the partial correlation analyses for personality characteristics and the three dimensions of the good working life are shown in Table 4.2. The findings on the personality correlates are also graphically summarized in Fig. 4.1. As expected, job satisfaction was strongly and positively related to emotional stability and conscientiousness and moderately and positively related to agreeableness. Moreover, job satisfaction was weakly and positively related to extraversion, whereas there was no significant association between job satisfaction and openness to experience. These findings are largely consistent with previous meta-analytic work (Judge et al., 2002).

Regarding work meaningfulness, previous empirical studies found positive, yet rather weak associations with assertiveness (a facet of extraversion) and industriousness (a facet of conscientiousness) (Woods & Sofat, 2013),

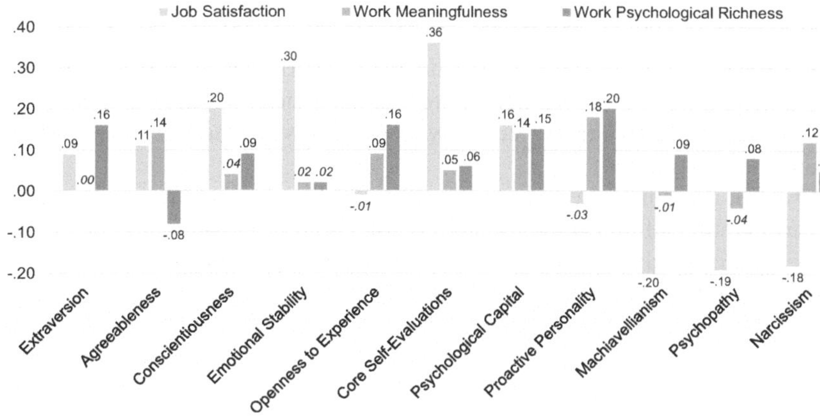

Fig. 4.1 Partial correlations between personality characteristics and dimensions of the good working life

as well as with extraversion, conscientiousness, and openness to experience (Frieder et al., 2018). However, these studies did not account for the substantial overlap between work meaningfulness and job satisfaction. Nevertheless, I expected that extraversion, conscientiousness, and openness to experience would also be positively associated with work meaningfulness in the empirical study conducted for this book. As shown in Table 4.2, openness to experience and agreeableness related weakly and positively to work meaningfulness, whereas extraversion, conscientiousness, and emotional stability did not have significant effects. These surprising findings, which are only partially consistent with expectations and previous studies, suggest that further theoretical and empirical research on the Big Five personality characteristics and work meaningfulness is needed.

Finally, initial research on individual difference predictors showed that living a psychologically rich life is associated with higher curiosity, more holistic thinking, and a more liberal political orientation (Oishi & Westgate, 2022). Accordingly, I expected that openness to experience, which entails intellectual curiosity, active imagination, and preference for variety (McCrae & Costa, 1997), is positively related to work psychological richness. Moreover, I expected an association between work psychological richness and extraversion, which reflects the tendency to be outgoing, sociable, and energetic and, therefore, might put people in work situations characterized by greater psychological richness. In contrast, I did not expect strong relations between work psychological richness and the other Big Five personality characteristics. Table 4.2 shows that, indeed, both openness to experience and extraversion were weakly and positively related to work psychological richness. Additionally, work psychological richness was also weakly and positively related to conscientiousness and weakly negatively related to agreeableness, whereas it was not significantly related to emotional stability.

Overall, these findings suggest that the Big Five personality characteristics contribute differentially to each of the three dimensions of the good working life. Higher levels of extraversion and conscientiousness seem to benefit both job satisfaction and work psychological richness but not work meaningfulness. Workers with higher levels of agreeableness tend to be more satisfied with their jobs and experience their work as more meaningful, but also as less psychologically rich. Higher emotional stability benefits only job satisfaction (but not work meaningfulness and psychological richness). Finally, openness to experience is only beneficial for work meaningfulness and psychological richness, but not for job satisfaction.

Core Self-Evaluations, Psychological Capital, and Proactive Personality

In addition to the Big Five personality characteristics, I assessed workers' core self-evaluations, psychological capital, and proactive personality in the empirical study conducted for this book. Core self-evaluations refer to a higher-order personality construct that combines high levels of generalized self-efficacy, self-esteem, emotional stability, and internal locus of control (Judge, 2009; Judge et al., 2003). Psychological capital is also a higher-order trait composed of the dimensions of hope, efficacy, resilience, and optimism (Lorenz et al., 2022; Luthans et al., 2007). Finally, proactive personality reflects people's dispositional tendency to take personal initiative and to initiate constructive change in the work environment (Crant, 1995).

Meta-analytic studies have reported positive associations between job satisfaction and core self-evaluations (Judge & Bono, 2001), psychological capital (Avey et al., 2011), and proactive personality (Spitzmuller et al., 2015). However, the unique relations between job satisfaction and these personality characteristics, controlling for work meaningfulness and psychological richness, have so far not been investigated. Nevertheless, consistent with previous research, I expected that job satisfaction would be positively related to core self-evaluations, psychological capital, and proactive personality. Previous research has demonstrated relations between core self-evaluations and work meaningfulness (Bipp, 2010), whereas the associations between psychological capital, proactive personality, and work meaningfulness are less clear. Likewise, these personality characteristics have not yet been investigated in relation to work psychological richness. Given that workers with a proactive personality tend to initiate constructive change in their environment, I expected a positive association between proactive personality and work psychological richness.

As shown in Table 4.2 and graphically illustrated in Fig. 4.1, core self-evaluations were, consistent with expectations, strongly and positively related to job satisfaction, as well as very weakly and positively related to work meaningfulness and psychological richness. Psychological capital was weakly and positively associated with all three dimensions of the good working life, whereas proactive personality was moderately and positively related to both work meaningfulness and psychological richness but not significantly related to job satisfaction. Overall, these findings suggest that the three compound personality constructs of core self-evaluations, psychological capital, and proactive personality are differentially related to the three dimensions of the good working life. Whereas core self-evaluations mattered most for job satisfaction, proactive personality was only relevant for work meaningfulness and psychological richness. Psychological capital, meanwhile, was positively associated with all three dimensions of the good working life, although the strength of these associations was relatively weak.

Dark Triad Traits

In contrast to the "bright-side" Big Five personality characteristics, core self-evaluations, psychological capital, and proactive personality, the dark triad traits include the undesirable characteristics of Machiavellianism (i.e., the tendency to manipulate and exploit others), psychopathy (i.e., the tendency to show antisocial behavior, impulsivity, thrill seeking, and callousness), and narcissism (i.e., the tendency to demonstrate grandiosity, entitlement, dominance, and superiority) (Jonason & Webster, 2010; Paulhus & Williams, 2002). Previous research has found positive relations between narcissism and job satisfaction, negative relations between psychopathy and job satisfaction, and non-significant relations between Machiavellianism and job satisfaction (Szabó et al., 2023). However, this research did not control for the other two dimensions of the good working life, and the associations between the dark triad traits and work meaningfulness and work psychological richness, respectively, have so far not received research attention. Accordingly, I did not have strong *a priori* assumptions about the unique relations between dark traits and the three dimensions of the good working life.

As shown in Table 4.2 and Fig. 4.1, all the three dark triad traits were moderately and negatively related to job satisfaction and weakly and positively related to work psychological richness. Only narcissism was positively related to work meaningfulness, whereas Machiavellianism and psychopathy were not significantly associated with meaningfulness. These differential findings on unique associations between the dark triad traits and the dimensions of the good working life suggest that workers with high levels of the dark triad traits enjoy their job generally less than workers with lower levels of these traits, but they perceive their work as more interesting, emotionally complex, and perspective-changing. Workers who are more narcissistic also perceive their work as more meaningful than those who are narcissistic.

Use of Character Strengths at Work

Table 4.3 provides an overview of the 24 character strengths (classified into six human virtues) and the three job crafting behaviors that I considered as potential antecedents of the good working life in the study conducted for this book. The table presents definitions, example items, response formats, reliability estimates, and sources of the measures. I investigated both the extent to which workers possess 24 character strengths as well as the extent to which they make use of each of these strengths at work. I then examined the interaction between each character strength and its use in relation to each of the dimensions of the good working life.

Table 4.3 Use of character strengths and job crafting behaviors: definitions and operationalizations

Construct	*Definition*	*Example item (number of items in parentheses, unless single item)*	*Response format*	*Cronbach's alpha reliability*	*Source*
Character strengths and use of character strengths at work					
Virtue I: wisdom and knowledge	Cognitive strengths that entail the acquisition and use of knowledge (creativity, curiosity, judgment, love of learning, perspective)	"Creativity (originality, ingenuity): Creative people have a highly developed thinking about novel and productive ways to solve problems and often have creative and original ideas. They do not content themselves with conventional solutions if there are better solutions." (five single items)	To what extent does this characteristic describe you? (5-point scale ranging from 0 = *does not describe me at all* to 4 = *describes me very well*); How often do you use this characteristic at your workplace? (5-point scale ranging from 0 = *never* to 5 = *always*)	–	Peterson and Seligman (2004); Ruch et al. (2014)

(*continued*)

Table 4.3 (continued)

Construct	*Definition*	*Example item (number of items in parentheses, unless single item)*	*Response format*	*Cronbach's alpha reliability*	*Source*
Virtue II: courage	Emotional strengths that involve the exercise of will to accomplish goals in the face of opposition, external or internal (bravery, perseverance, honesty, zest)	"Bravery (valor): Brave and courageous people do not shrink from threat, challenge, difficulty or pain. They speak up for their opinions and convictions even if there is opposition." (four single items)	To what extent does this characteristic describe you? (5-point scale ranging from 0 = *does not describe me at all* to 4 = *describes me very well*); How often do you use this characteristic at your workplace? (5-point scale ranging from 0 = *never* to 5 = *always*)	–	Peterson and Seligman (2004); Ruch et al. (2014)
Virtue III: humanity	Interpersonal strengths that involve "tending and befriending" others (love, kindness, social intelligence)	"Capacity to Love and Be Loved: People with a highly developed capacity to love and a secure attachment value close relations with others, in particular those in which sharing and caring are reciprocated." (three single items)	To what extent does this characteristic describe you? (5-point scale ranging from 0 = *does not describe me at all* to 4 = *describes me very well*); How often do you use this characteristic at your workplace? (5-point scale ranging from 0 = *never* to 5 = *always*)	–	Peterson and Seligman (2004); Ruch et al. (2014)

(*continued*)

Table 4.3 (continued)

Construct	*Definition*	*Example item (number of items in parentheses, unless single item)*	*Response format*	*Cronbach's alpha reliability*	*Source*
Virtue IV: justice	Civic strengths that underlie healthy community life (teamwork, fairness, leadership)	"Teamwork (citizenship, social responsibility, loyalty): People with highly developed teamwork skills work well as a member of a group or team. They are loyal to the group and consider being a team member as a central factor." (three single items)	To what extent does this characteristic describe you? (5-point scale ranging from 0 = *does not describe me at all* to 4 = *describes me very well*); How often do you use this characteristic at your workplace? (5-point scale ranging from 0 = *never* to 5 = *always*)	–	Peterson and Seligman (2004); Ruch et al. (2014)
Virtue V: temperance	Strengths that protect against excess (forgiveness, modesty, prudence, self-regulation)	"Forgiveness & Mercy: People with this strength have an easier time forgiving those who have done wrong. They give people a second chance. Being merciful and not being vengeful is their principle." (four single items)	To what extent does this characteristic describe you? (5-point scale ranging from 0 = *does not describe me at all* to 4 = *describes me very well*); How often do you use this characteristic at your workplace? (5-point scale ranging from 0 = *never* to 5 = *always*)	–	Peterson and Seligman (2004); Ruch et al. (2014)

(*continued*)

Table 4.3 (continued)

Construct	*Definition*	*Example item (number of items in parentheses, unless single item)*	*Response format*	*Cronbach's alpha reliability*	*Source*
Virtue VI: transcendence	Strengths that forge connections to the larger universe and provide meaning (appreciation of beauty and excellence, gratitude, hope, humor, religiousness)	"Appreciation of Beauty and Excellence (awe, wonder, elevation): People with this strength notice and appreciate things. They are highly interested in beauty, excellence, and/or skilled performance in various domains of life (from nature to art to mathematics to science to everyday experience)." (five single items)	To what extent does this characteristic describe you? (5-point scale ranging from 0 = *does not describe me at all* to 4 = *describes me very well*); How often do you use this characteristic at your workplace? (5-point scale ranging from 0 = *never* to 5 = *always*)	–	Peterson and Seligman (2004); Ruch et al. (2014)
Job crafting behaviors					
Task crafting	Behavior that involves actively changing the tasks one has to complete at work (e.g., taking on more or fewer tasks, changing the scope of the tasks, changing the means of task accomplishment)	"So that the job I do suits me ... I concentrate on specific tasks." (3)	5-point Likert scale ranging from 1 = *strongly disagree* to 5 = *strongly agree*	0.87	Niessen et al. (2016)

(*continued*)

Table 4.3 (continued)

Construct	*Definition*	*Example item (number of items in parentheses, unless single item)*	*Response format*	*Cronbach's alpha reliability*	*Source*
Relational crafting	Behavior that involves changing the amount and/or quality of interactions with other people at work (e.g., supervisors, coworkers, customers)	"So that the job I do suits me … I usually limit the amount of time I spend with people I do not get along well with, and only contact them for things that are absolutely necessary." (3)	5-point Likert scale ranging from 1 = *strongly disagree* to 5 = *strongly agree*	0.74	Niessen et al. (2016)
Cognitive crafting	Behavior that involves reframing how one perceives one's job and changing the cognitive representation of one's job	"So that the job I do suits me … I try to look upon the tasks and responsibilities I have at work as having a deeper meaning than is readily apparent." (3)	5-point Likert scale ranging from 1 = *strongly disagree* to 5 = *strongly agree*	0.87	Niessen et al. (2016)

Character strengths are positive and morally desirable human characteristics that can be classified into six universal virtues (Peterson & Seligman, 2004).

First, the virtue of ***wisdom and knowledge*** entails five cognitive strengths related to the acquisition and use of knowledge (Peterson & Seligman, 2004; Ruch et al., 2014):

(1) Creativity: Thinking of novel and useful ways to do things,
(2) Curiosity: Taking an interest in all ongoing experience,
(3) Judgment: Thinking things through and examining them from different perspectives,
(4) Love of learning: Mastering new bodies of knowledge and skills, and
(5) Perspective: Being able to provide wise counsel to other people.

Second, the virtue of *courage* involves four emotional strengths, especially the exercise of will to accomplish goals in the face of internal or external opposition (Peterson & Seligman, 2004; Ruch et al., 2014):

(6) Bravery: Not avoiding threat, challenge, difficulty, or pain,
(7) Perseverance: Finishing what one has started,
(8) Honesty: Speaking the truth and presenting oneself in a genuine way, and
(9) Zest: Approaching life with excitement and energy.

Third, the virtue of *humanity* entails three interpersonal strengths related to tending and befriending other people (Peterson & Seligman, 2004; Ruch et al., 2014):

(10) Love: Valuing close relations with others,
(11) Kindness: Doing favors and good deeds for others, and
(12) Social intelligence: Being aware of the needs and feelings of self and others.

Fourth, the virtue of *justice* includes three civic strengths that underlie healthy community life (Peterson & Seligman, 2004; Ruch et al., 2014):

(13) Teamwork: Working well as a member of a group or team,
(14) Fairness: Treating all people the same way in line with notions of justice, and
(15) Leadership: Organizing group activities and making sure that they happen.

Fifth, the virtue of *temperance* includes four strengths that protect against excess (Peterson & Seligman, 2004; Ruch et al., 2014):

(16) Forgiveness: Forgiving those who have done wrong,
(17) Modesty: Letting one's accomplishments speak for themselves,
(18) Prudence: Being careful about one's choices; not saying or doing things that might later be regretted, and
(19) Self-regulation: psychologically regulating what one feels and does.

Finally, the virtue of transcendence includes five strengths that forge connections to the larger universe and provide meaning (Peterson & Seligman, 2004; Ruch et al., 2014):

(20) Appreciation of beauty and excellence: Noticing and valuing beauty, excellence, and/or skilled performance in all domains of life,
(21) Gratitude: Being aware of and thankful for the good things that happen in life,
(22) Hope: Expecting the best and working to achieve it,
(23) Humor: Enjoying to laugh and joke; bringing smiles to other people, and
(24) Spirituality/religiousness: Having coherent beliefs about the higher purpose and meaning of life.

Table 4.4 shows the results of several multiple regression analyses used to test the effects of (a) the extent to which workers possess each of the character strengths (i.e., the first estimate in each cell), (b) the actual use of each character strength at work (i.e., the second estimate in each cell), and (c) the interaction effect of the possession and use of each character strength (i.e., the third estimate in each cell) on each of the three dimensions of the good working life, while controlling for the respective other two dimensions. I used a different analytical approach for the use of character strengths at work, because workers' possession of a specific character strength and the use of this strength at work can only be interpreted in combination. The possession of a strength itself is not relevant for the good working life if a worker does not make use of it at work, and the application of a strength is not possible if a worker does not possess it. Thus, to examine the combined and unique effects of the possession and use of different character strengths on each dimension of the good working life, significant partial correlations are not sufficient; a significant interaction effect is needed.

Figure 4.2 illustrates the significant interaction effect between the character strength "appreciation of beauty" and the use of this particular strength at work on work psychological richness. The interaction pattern suggests that workers' possession of the strength only has a significant effect on work psychological richness if workers also make use of this strength (i.e., the diagonal dashed line represents a positive effect). In contrast, workers' possession of the strength does not have a significant effect on work psychological richness if they do not make use of that

Table 4.4 Standardized regression coefficients for the effects of character strengths (first coefficient in each cell), use of character strengths at work (second coefficient), and their respective interactions (third coefficient), as well as partial correlations between job crafting and dimensions of the good working life (corrected for the respective other two dimensions of the good working life)

	Job satisfaction	*Work meaningfulness*	*Work psychological richness*
Virtue I: wisdom and knowledge			
Creativity	**(0.03)/(0.03)/0.08**	(0.02)/(0.02)/(−0.01)	**(0.01)/0.17/0.03**
Curiosity	**0.04/0.05/0.05**	(0.02)/0.04/(0.01)	**(0.01)/0.12/0.05**
Judgment	**0.05/(0.02)/0.05**	(0.01)/0.05/(0.02)	(0.01)/0.10/(0.01)
Love of learning	**(0.02)/0.07/0.07**	(0.01)/0.07/(0.01)	(0.01)/0.11/(0.03)
Perspective	**(0.01)/(0.04)/0.06**	(0.01)/0.05/(0.001)	(0.02)/0.10/(0.01)
Virtue II: courage			
Bravery	**(0.001)/−0.04/0.04**	(0.02)/0.04/(0.01)	0.04/0.10/(0.02)
Perseverance	0.09/(0.04)/(0.03)	(−0.01)/0.04/(0.01)	(0.02)/0.07/(0.01)
Honesty	**(0.02)/0.14/0.04**	(−0.003)/(0.03)/(0.02)	(0.02)/0.04/(−0.01)
Zest	0.05/0.12/(0.01)	(0.02)/0.06/(0.02)	0.04/0.06/(0.02)
Virtue III: humanity			
Love	0.05/(−0.003)/(0.03)	(0.02)/0.05/(−0.02)	**(0.01)/0.10/0.04**
Kindness	(0.04)/0.08/(0.03)	(0.01)/0.03/(−0.01)	**(−0.001)/0.06/0.04**
Social intelligence	(0.004)/0.07/(0.03)	(−0.01)/0.04/(−0.01)	**0.05/0.10/0.05**
Virtue IV: justice			
Teamwork	**0.04/0.08/0.10**	(0.03)/(−0.02)/−0.05	**(−0.01)/0.07/0.04**
Fairness	**0.05/0.12/0.04**	(−0.02)/0.03/(−0.01)	**(0.03)/0.05/0.04**
Leadership	**0.06/(−0.01)/0.06**	(0.03)/(0.02)/(−0.01)	(0.03)/0.09/(0.02)
Virtue V: temperance			
Forgiveness	0.06/−0.04/(0.02)	0.03/(0.02)/(−0.02)	**(0.002)/0.08/0.05**
Modesty	0.04/(−0.03)/(0.03)	(0.01)/0.04/(−0.01)	**(−0.02)/0.05/0.04**
Prudence	(0.02)/−0.04/(0.02)	(0.004)/0.04/(−0.03)	**(−0.01)/0.05/0.06**
Self-regulation	(0.004)/(−0.02)/(0.02)	0.06/(0.01)/(−0.01)	**(−0.02)/0.08/0.03**

Virtue VI: transcendence			
Appreciation of beauty	**(0.03)/−0.07/0.07**	(0.03)/0.05/−0.03	**(0.02)/0.09/0.06**
Gratitude	**0.07/(0.03)/0.04**	(0.002)/0.06/−0.03	**(0.01)/0.06/0.06**
Hope	0.09/(0.02)/(0.03)	0.04/0.05/(0.02)	(−0.02)/0.10/(−0.002)
Humor	**0.05/(0.02)/0.04**	(−0.01)/(0.01)/(−0.01)	(0.01)/0.10/(0.02)
Spirituality/religiousness	(−0.02)/−0.09/(0.01)	0.03/(0.03)/(0.02)	(0.002)/0.05/(0.01)
Job crafting			
Task crafting[a]	0.09	0.23	0.09
Relational crafting[a]	(−0.05)	0.10	0.13
Cognitive crafting[a]	(0.001)	0.35	0.10

Note: N = Due to missing data, N ranged from 2058 to 2059

[a] N = 1325 to 1328 (assessed at Time 2). Non-significant correlations ($p > 0.05$) are shown in parentheses. Estimates in cells with significant interaction effects (between character strengths and use of character strengths at work) are highlighted in bold

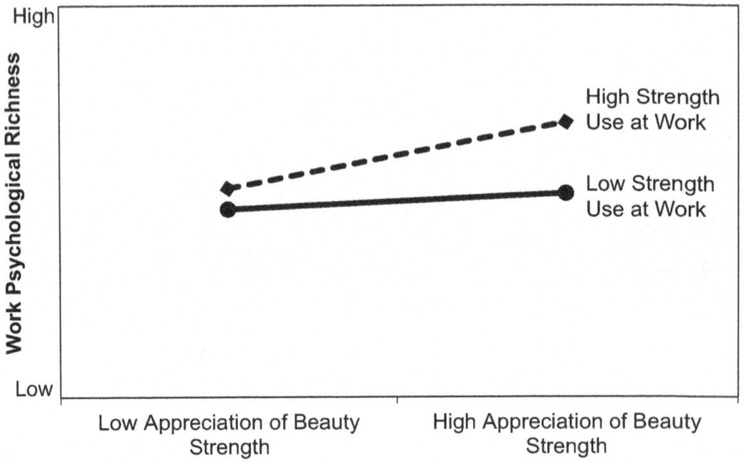

Fig. 4.2 Interaction effect of possessing and using the character strength "appreciation of beauty" on work psychological richness

strength at work (i.e., the relatively flat solid line represents a non-significant effect).

The results presented in Table 4.4 suggest that workers' use of character strengths belonging to the virtue of wisdom and knowledge (i.e., creativity, curiosity, judgment, love of learning, and perspective) primarily benefits their job satisfaction. However, the use of the character strengths of creativity and curiosity also predicted higher levels of work psychological richness. The use of wisdom and knowledge strengths generally did not significantly affect work meaningfulness.

The use of two specific character strengths that belong to the virtue of courage, namely bravery and honesty, predicted higher levels of job satisfaction, whereas perseverance and zest did not have significant effects. There were also no significant interaction effects on work meaningfulness and psychological richness.

The use of all three character strengths belonging to the virtue of humanity (i.e., love, kindness, social intelligence) predicted higher levels of work psychological richness, whereas the use of these strengths did not significantly predict job satisfaction and work meaningfulness.

The use of all three character strengths belonging to the virtue of justice (i.e., teamwork, fairness, leadership) predicted higher levels of job satisfaction and, with the exception of leadership, also higher levels of work psychological richness. In contrast, the use of these character strengths did not significantly predict work meaningfulness.

The use of all four character strengths that belong to the virtue of temperance (i.e., forgiveness, modesty, prudence, self-regulation) predicted higher levels of work psychological richness. In contrast, the use of these character strengths did not significantly predict job satisfaction and work meaningfulness.

Finally, the use of three character strengths that belong to the virtue of transcendence (i.e., appreciation of beauty, gratitude, humor) predicted higher levels of job satisfaction, and the use of appreciation of beauty and gratitude also predicted higher work psychological richness (see Fig. 4.2 for a graphical illustration of the interaction effect between the possession and use of "appreciation of beauty" on work psychological richness).

In summary, the findings on the use of character strengths at work suggest that workers are likely to achieve higher levels of job satisfaction if they possess and make use of character strengths associated with the virtues of wisdom and knowledge and justice, as well as select strengths from the virtues of courage and transcendence. Furthermore, workers are likely to achieve higher levels of work psychological richness if they possess and make use of character strengths associated with the virtues of humanity and temperance, as well as select strengths from the virtues of wisdom and knowledge, justice, and transcendence. Finally, the findings also suggest that the use of character strengths at work does not significantly predict work meaningfulness. Especially the latter findings are surprising and require further research on the use of character strengths at work and the three dimensions of the good working life.

Job Crafting Behaviors

In addition to the rather stable personality characteristics (e.g., Big Five, dark triad traits, core self-evaluations) and workers' use of character strengths, I also examined the unique associations between workers' individual job crafting behaviors and each of the three dimensions of the good working life in the empirical study conducted for this book. Job crafting refers to a form of proactive work behavior that comprises intentional changes workers make to different aspects of their work role, such as asking for and taking on new and challenging projects, seeking out new collaborations and strengthening positive relationships with coworkers, or thinking about their work in a different way that highlights its meaningfulness (Niessen et al., 2016; Rudolph et al., 2017; Wrzesniewski & Dutton, 2001).

Three broad dimensions of job crafting behavior can be distinguished: first, task crafting involves that workers make active changes to their work tasks, for example, by taking on more or fewer tasks, changing the scope of their tasks, or changing the ways in which they work to complete the tasks. Second, relational crafting entails that workers make active changes to the quantity or quality of their social relationships and interactions with other people at their workplace, including coworkers, supervisors, clients, and customers. Third, cognitive crafting involves that workers actively change how they think about their jobs and their meaning. For example, workers may reframe the meaning of their work by considering how they contribute to other people and society by accomplishing their work tasks (Wrzesniewski & Dutton, 2001).

Previous research has demonstrated positive associations between job crafting and job satisfaction (Rudolph et al., 2017) as well as work meaningfulness (Tims et al., 2016). In contrast, previous research has not yet examined the unique associations between job crafting and job satisfaction and work meaningfulness, respectively (i.e., controlling for the respective other two dimensions of the good working life), and so far, there is no research on job crafting and work psychological richness. Consistent with previous research, I expected generally positive unique associations between the three job crafting dimensions and both job satisfaction and work meaningfulness. Additionally, given that job crafting involves proactive and constructive changes to the work role (and how workers think about their work), I expected that it is also linked to greater work psychological richness.

As shown in Table 4.4, only task crafting was positively related to job satisfaction, whereas relational and cognitive crafting was not significantly related to job satisfaction. All three dimensions of job crafting were positively related to work meaningfulness, with cognitive crafting being the strongest unique correlate of meaningfulness, followed by task and relational crafting. Finally, all three job crafting dimensions were positively, albeit relatively weakly, associated with work psychological richness. Overall, these findings on unique associations between job crafting and the good working life extend previous research by suggesting that job crafting generally matters more for work meaningfulness (especially cognitive crafting) and work psychological richness, whereas it has a lesser impact on job satisfaction.

Summary

The results presented in this chapter suggest that various individual characteristics uniquely and differentially relate to the three dimensions of the good working life. Whereas demographic characteristics, such as age, sex, and education, had only relatively weak or non-significant associations with the good working life, several personality characteristics had significant associations with job satisfaction, work meaningfulness, and work psychological richness. Specifically, extraversion, agreeableness, conscientiousness, and emotional stability, as well as core self-evaluations and psychological capital, were associated with higher job satisfaction, whereas Machiavellianism, psychopathy, and narcissism were related to lower job satisfaction. Agreeableness, openness to experience, psychological capital, proactive personality and, surprisingly, narcissism were related to higher work meaningfulness. Extraversion, openness to experience, psychological capital, proactive personality, and all the dark triad traits predicted higher work psychological richness. In contrast, agreeableness was negatively related to work psychological richness, suggesting that friendly and kind workers have somewhat less interesting work experiences. Only psychological capital was moderately and positively related to all three dimensions of the good working life, suggesting that the combination of dispositional hope, efficacy, resilience, and optimism generally contributes to the good working life.

The use of specific character strengths, and even applying entire classes of virtues, at work can also contribute to a good working life. Specifically, the possession and use of character strengths associated with the virtues of wisdom and knowledge and justice, as well as select strengths from the virtues of courage and transcendence, were associated with higher job satisfaction. The possession and use of character strengths associated with the virtues of humanity and temperance, as well as select strengths from the virtues of wisdom and knowledge, justice, and transcendence, were linked to higher work psychological richness. Surprisingly, however, the possession and use of character strengths at work did not significantly predict work meaningfulness. Finally, job crafting behaviors that involve making active and constructive changes to one's work tasks, social relationships at work, and one's own cognitive representations of the job were positively related to work psychological richness and (for task and cognitive crafting) work meaningfulness, but not job satisfaction.

References

Avey, J. B., Reichard, R. J., Luthans, F., & Mhatre, K. H. (2011). Meta-analysis of the impact of positive psychological capital on employee attitudes, behaviors, and performance. *Human Resource Development Quarterly, 22*(2), 127–152. https://doi.org/10.1002/hrdq.20070

Barrick, M. R., Mount, M. K., & Li, N. (2013). The theory of purposeful work behavior: The role of personality, job characteristics, and experienced meaningfulness. *Academy of Management Review, 38*(1), 132–153. https://doi.org/10.5465/amr.2010.0479

Bipp, T. (2010). What do people want from their jobs? The Big Five, core self-evaluations and work motivation. *International Journal of Selection and Assessment, 18*(1), 28–39. https://doi.org/10.1111/j.1468-2389.2010.00486.x

Carstensen, L. L., Isaacowitz, D. M., & Charles, S. T. (1999). Taking time seriously: A theory of socioemotional selectivity. *American Psychologist, 54*(3), 165–181. https://doi.org/10.1037/0003-066X.54.3.165

Crant, J. M. (1995). The Proactive Personality Scale and objective job performance among real estate agents. *Journal of Applied Psychology, 80*(4), 532–537. https://doi.org/10.1037/0021-9010.80.4.532

Digman, J. M. (1990). Personality structure: Emergence of the five-factor model. *Annual Review of Psychology, 41*, 417–440. https://doi.org/10.1146/annurev.ps.41.020190.002221

Frieder, R. E., Wang, G., & Oh, I.-S. (2018). Linking job-relevant personality traits, transformational leadership, and job performance via perceived meaningfulness at work: A moderated mediation model. *Journal of Applied Psychology, 103*(3), 324–333. https://doi.org/10.1037/apl0000274

Jonason, P. K., & Webster, G. D. (2010). The dirty dozen: A concise measure of the dark triad. *Psychological Assessment, 22*(2), 420–432. https://doi.org/10.1037/a0019265

Judge, T. A. (2009). Core self-evaluations and work success. *Current Directions in Psychological Science, 18*(1), 58–62. https://doi.org/10.1111/j.1467-8721.2009.01606.x

Judge, T. A., & Bono, J. E. (2001). Relationship of core self-evaluations traits – self-esteem, generalized self-efficacy, locus of control, and emotional stability – with job satisfaction and job performance: A meta-analysis. *Journal of Applied Psychology, 86*(1), 80–92. https://doi.org/10.1037/0021-9010.86.1.80

Judge, T. A., Erez, A., Bono, J. E., & Thoresen, C. J. (2003). The Core Self-Evaluations Scale (CSES): Development of a measure. *Personnel Psychology, 56*, 303–331. https://doi.org/10.1111/j.1744-6570.2003.tb00152.x

Judge, T. A., Heller, D., & Mount, M. K. (2002). Five-factor model of personality and job satisfaction: A meta-analysis. *Journal of Applied Psychology, 87*(3), 530–541. https://doi.org/10.1037/0021-9010.87.3.530

Judge, T. A., & Kammeyer-Mueller, J. D. (2012). Job attitudes. *Annual Review of Psychology, 63*, 341–367. https://doi.org/10.1146/annurev-psych-120710-100511

Küfner, A. C., Dufner, M., & Back, M. D. (2014). Das Dreckige Dutzend und die Niederträchtigen Neun: Kurzskalen zur Erfassung von Narzissmus, Machiavellismus und Psychopathie [The Dirty Dozen and the Naughty Nine: Short scales for the assessment of narcissism, Machiavellianism, and psychopathy]. *Diagnostica, 61*(2), 76–91. https://doi.org/10.1026/0012-1924/a000124

Lorenz, T., Hagitte, L., & Prasath, P. R. (2022). Validation of the revised Compound PsyCap Scale (CPC-12R) and its measurement invariance across the US and Germany. *Frontiers in Psychology, 13*, 1075031. https://doi.org/10.3389/fpsyg.2022.1075031

Luthans, F., Avolio, B. J., Avey, J. B., & Norman, S. M. (2007). Positive psychological capital: Measurement and relationship with performance and satisfaction. *Personnel Psychology, 60*(3), 541–572. https://doi.org/10.1111/j.1744-6570.2007.00083.x

McCrae, R. R., & Costa, P. T., Jr. (1997). Personality trait structure as a human universal. *American Psychologist, 52*(5), 509–516. https://doi.org/10.1037/0003-066X.52.5.509

Ng, T. W. H., & Feldman, D. C. (2010). The relationship of age with job attitudes: A meta-analysis. *Personnel Psychology, 63*(3), 667–718. https://doi.org/10.1111/j.1744-6570.2010.01184.x

Niessen, C., Weseler, D., & Kostova, P. (2016). When and why do individuals craft their jobs? The role of individual motivation and work characteristics for job crafting. *Human Relations, 69*(6), 1287–1313. https://doi.org/10.1177/0018726715610642

Oishi, S., & Westgate, E. C. (2022). A psychologically rich life: Beyond happiness and meaning. *Psychological Review, 129*(4), 790–811. https://doi.org/10.1037/rev0000317

Paulhus, D. L., & Williams, K. M. (2002). The dark triad of personality: Narcissism, Machiavellianism, and psychopathy. *Journal of Research in Personality, 36*(6), 556–563. https://doi.org/10.1016/S0092-6566(02)00505-6

Peterson, C., & Seligman, M. E. P. (2004). *Character strengths and virtues: A handbook and classification*. American Psychological Association.

Rammstedt, B., & John, O. P. (2005). Kurzversion des Big Five Inventory (BFI-K) [Short version of the Big Five Inventory (BFI-K)]. *Diagnostica, 51*(4), 195–206. https://doi.org/10.1026/0012-1924.51.4.195

Ruch, W., Martínez-Martí, M. L., Proyer, R. T., & Harzer, C. (2014). The Character Strengths Rating Form (CSRF): Development and initial assessment of a 24-item rating scale to assess character strengths. *Personality and Individual Differences, 68*, 53–58. https://doi.org/10.1016/j.paid.2014.03.042

Rudolph, C. W., Katz, I. M., Lavigne, K. N., & Zacher, H. (2017). Job crafting: A meta-analysis of relationships with individual differences, job characteristics, and work outcomes. *Journal of Vocational Behavior, 102*, 112–138. https://doi.org/10.1016/j.jvb.2017.05.008

Rudolph, C. W., Kooij, D. T. A. M., Rauvola, R. S., & Zacher, H. (2018). Occupational future time perspective: A meta-analysis of antencedents and outcomes. *Journal of Organizational Behavior, 39*(2), 229–248. https://doi.org/10.1002/job.2264

Schwall, A. R. (2012). Defining age and using age-relevant constructs. In J. W. Hedge & W. C. Borman (Eds.), *The Oxford Handbook of Work and Aging (pp. 169-186)*. Oxford University Press. https://doi.org/10.1093/oxfordhb/9780195385052.013.0080

Seibert, S. E., Crant, J. M., & Kraimer, M. L. (1999). Proactive personality and career success. *Journal of Applied Psychology, 84*, 416–427. https://doi.org/10.1037/0021-9010.84.3.416

Spitzmuller, M., Sin, H. P., Howe, M., & Fatimah, S. (2015). Investigating the uniqueness and usefulness of proactive personality in organizational research: A meta-analytic review. *Human Performance, 28*(4), 351–379. https://doi.org/10.1080/08959285.2015.1021041

Staudinger, U. M., & Kunzmann, U. (2005). Positive adult personality development: Adjustment and/or growth? *European Psychologist, 10*(4), 320–329. https://doi.org/10.1027/1016-9040.10.4.320

Szabó, Z. P., Diller, S. J., Czibor, A., Restás, P., Jonas, E., & Frey, D. (2023). "One of these things is not like the others": The associations between dark triad personality traits, work attitudes, and work-related motivation. *Personality and Individual Differences, 205*, 112098. https://doi.org/10.1016/j.paid.2023.112098

Tims, M., Derks, D., & Bakker, A. B. (2016). Job crafting and its relationships with person–job fit and meaningfulness: A three-wave study. *Journal of Vocational Behavior, 92*, 44–53. https://doi.org/10.1016/j.jvb.2015.11.007

Van der Linden, D., Pekaar, K. A., Bakker, A. B., Schermer, J. A., Vernon, P. A., Dunkel, C. S., & Petrides, K. V. (2017). Overlap between the general factor of personality and emotional intelligence: A meta-analysis. *Psychological Bulletin, 143*(1), 1939–1455. https://doi.org/10.1037/bul0000078

Woods, S. A., & Sofat, J. A. (2013). Personality and engagement at work: The mediating role of psychological meaningfulness. *Journal of Applied Social Psychology, 43*(11), 2203–2210. https://doi.org/10.1111/jasp.12171

Wrzesniewski, A., & Dutton, J. E. (2001). Crafting a job: Revisioning employees as active crafters of their work. *Academy of Management Review, 26*(2), 179–201. https://doi.org/10.5465/AMR.2001.4378011

Zacher, H., & Frese, M. (2009). Remaining time and opportunities at work: Relationships between age, work characteristics, and occupational future time perspective. *Psychology and Aging, 24*(2), 487–493. https://doi.org/10.1037/a0015425

CHAPTER 5

Work Characteristics and the Good Working Life

Abstract In this chapter, I examine relations between various work-related characteristics, including key employment characteristics (e.g., industry), job stressors, and job resources, and the three dimensions of the good working life. Employment characteristics were generally only weakly associated with the good working life. However, job satisfaction, work meaningfulness, and work psychological richness differed significantly across industries. Job stressors, such as quantitative and emotional work demands, work privacy conflicts, job insecurity, role conflicts, and unfair treatment, were generally negatively associated with job satisfaction but positively associated with work psychological richness. Most job stressors were not significantly related to work meaningfulness. In contrast, most job resources, such as influence at work, possibilities for development, predictability of work, quality of leadership, feedback, and recognition, were positively related to all three dimensions of the good working life.

Keywords Work characteristics • Employment • Industry • Job stressors • Job resources

In which employment situations and jobs are workers more likely or less likely to experience high levels of job satisfaction, work meaningfulness, and work psychological richness? The goal of this chapter is to examine

H. Zacher, *The Good Working Life*,
https://doi.org/10.1007/978-3-031-77221-4_5

relations between various work-related characteristics, including key employment characteristics (e.g., industry, income, work hours), job stressors, and job resources, and the three dimensions of the good working life. Table 5.1 provides an overview of the potential employment- and job-related antecedents of the good working life investigated in the empirical study conducted for this book, including definitions, example items, response formats, reliability estimates, and sources of the measures.

Employment Characteristics

I examined relations between the three dimensions of the good working life and ten employment characteristics, including job tenure, job level, income, financial difficulties, industry, supervisory status, work hours, shift work, contract type, and working from home (see Table 5.1). Except for work hours, job level, working from home, and financial difficulties, these characteristics were not included in the study by Zacher and Baumeister (2024), which focused on job stressors and job resources. Specifically, these authors found that work hours were weakly positively related to work meaningfulness, job level was weakly positively related to job satisfaction and work psychological richness, working from home was weakly positively related to job satisfaction, and financial difficulties were negatively related to job satisfaction and positively related to work psychological richness. Based on these initial findings, I did not have strong expectations for the new empirical study conducted for this book regarding the relations between employment characteristics and the three dimensions of the good working life.

The results of the partial correlations between employment characteristics and the three dimensions of the good working life are shown in Table 5.2. Overall, these correlations were either very weak or non-significant. An exception was the moderate and negative correlation between job satisfaction and financial difficulties, which replicates the finding by Zacher and Baumeister (2024). Additionally, job satisfaction was weakly positively related to job level and weakly negatively related to work hours and shift work. However, the positive association between working from home and job satisfaction found by Zacher and Baumeister (2024) was not replicated in the study conducted for this book, which may be explained by research showing that working from home can have both positive (e.g., increased autonomy) and negative effects (e.g., professional isolation), and that high levels of working from home may

Table 5.1 Work characteristics: definitions and operationalizations

Construct	*Definition*	*Example item (number of items in parentheses, unless single item)*	*Response format*	*Cronbach's alpha reliability*	*Source*
Employment characteristics					
Job tenure	Amount of time worked in the current job	"How long have you worked in your current job (in years)?"	Open answer	–	–
Job level	Position in the organizational hierarchy	"Please indicate your position in your organization on a ladder with seven ranks."	7-point scale (1 = *entry level position*, 7 = *executive position*)	–	von Hippel et al. (2013)
Income	Personal net salary per month	"What is your personal net income per month?"	Open answer	–	–
Financial difficulties	Difficulties covering ongoing costs of living	"Did you have problems lately covering your ongoing costs (e.g., buying groceries, rent, bills)?"	5-point scale (1 = *never*, 5 = *always*)	–	Caleyachetty et al. (2012)
Industry	Branch of economic activity related to one's job	"In which industry do you currently work?"	21 options (see Fig. 5.1)	–	Eurostat (2008)
Supervisory status	Supervisory responsibility for other people at work	"Do you have supervisory responsibility in your position?"	1 = no, 2 = yes		–

(*continued*)

Table 5.1 (continued)

Construct	*Definition*	*Example item (number of items in parentheses, unless single item)*	*Response format*	*Cronbach's alpha reliability*	*Source*
Work hours	Number of actual hours worked on average per week	"How many hours do you actually work per week, on average?"	Open answer	–	–
Shift work	Chronology of work time	"What best describes your work situation?"	1 = day work, 2 = shift work	–	–
Contract type	Duration of one's work contract	"Your current work contract is …?"	1 = permanent, 2 = temporary	–	–
Working from home	Amount of time per week that one actually works from home	"What percentage of your work time do you work from home, on average?"	Slider from 0% to 100%	–	Rudolph and Zacher (2024)
Job stressors					
Quantitative demands	The quantity of tasks one has to achieve at work; incompatibility between the amount of tasks and the time available to perform these tasks successfully	"Do you have to work very fast?" (5)	5-point scale (1 = *never*, 5 = *always*)	0.83	Burr et al. (2019); Lincke et al. (2021)
Emotional demands	The requirement to deal with or being confronted with other people's feelings at work	"Do you have to deal with other people's personal problems as part of your work?" (2)	5-point scale (1 = *never*, 5 = *always*)	0.76	Burr et al. (2019); Lincke et al. (2021)
Hiding emotions	The requirement to conceal one's own feelings at work from other people	"Does your work require that you hide your feelings?" (2)	5-point scale (1 = *to a small extent*, 5 = *to a great extent*)	0.81	Burr et al. (2019); Lincke et al. (2021)

Work privacy conflicts	Negative consequences of work on personal and family life (e.g., conflict regarding time, and energy)	"The demands of my work interfere with my private and family life." (4)	5-point scale (1 = *to a small extent*, 5 = *to a great extent*)	0.92	Burr et al. (2019); Lincke et al. (2021)
Dissolution	Suspension of boundaries between work and private life	"I take care of work-related tasks outside of my working time as well." (2)	5-point scale (1 = *to a small extent*, 5 = *to a great extent*)	0.73	Burr et al. (2019); Lincke et al. (2021)
Role conflicts	Conflicting demands within a task and when prioritizing different tasks	"Are contradictory demands placed on you at work?" (3)	5-point scale (1 = *to a small extent*, 5 = *to a great extent*)	0.82	Burr et al. (2019); Lincke et al. (2021)
Unfair treatment	Extent to which one feels treated unfairly by others at work	"How often do you feel unjustly criticized, bullied, or shown up in front of others by your colleagues or your superior?"	5-point scale (1 = *never*, 5 = *always*)	–	Burr et al. (2019); Lincke et al. (2021)
Work environment/ physical demands	Environmental stressors, such as physical demands, noise, extreme temperatures, chemicals, poor air, and poor lighting	"How often do you have to do physically strenuous work such as lift, carry or raise heavy objects?" (6)	5-point scale (1 = *never*, 5 = *always*)	.	Burr et al. (2019); Lincke et al. (2021)
Job insecurity	Security of employment, including the risk of being fired or the certainty of being reemployed if fired	"Are you worried about becoming unemployed?" (3)	5-point scale (1 = *to a small extent*, 5 = *to a great extent*)	.	Burr et al. (2019); Lincke et al. (2021)

(*continued*)

Table 5.1 (continued)

Construct	*Definition*	*Example item (number of items in parentheses, unless single item)*	*Response format*	*Cronbach's alpha reliability*	*Source*
Insecurity over working conditions	Security of working conditions, including content of work, working hours, and pay	"Are you worried about being transferred to another job against your will?" (3)	5-point scale (1 = *to a small extent*, 5 = *to a great extent*)	.	Burr et al. (2019); Lincke et al. (2021)
Job resources					
Influence at work	Extent to which workers can influence aspects of their work, including planning of work and order of tasks	"Do you have a large degree of influence on the decisions concerning your work?" (3)	5-point scale (1 = *never*, 5 = *always*)	0.81	Burr et al. (2019); Lincke et al. (2021)
Degrees of freedom (breaks/ holidays)	Extent to which workers can influence their working conditions, such as breaks, length of the working day, or work schedules	"Can you decide when to take a break?" (2)	5-point scale (1 = *never*, 5 = *always*)	0.68	Burr et al. (2019); Lincke et al. (2021)
Possibilities for development	Extent to which tasks are challenging and provide opportunities for learning and development	"Do you have the possibility of learning new things through your work?" (3)	5-point scale (1 = *to a small extent*, 5 = *to a great extent*)	0.78	Burr et al. (2019); Lincke et al. (2021)
Predictability of work	Possibility to avoid uncertainty and insecurity through receiving relevant information at the right time	"At your place of work, are you informed well in advance concerning for example important decisions, changes, or plans for the future?" (2)	5-point scale (1 = *to a small extent*, 5 = *to a great extent*)	0.79	Burr et al. (2019); Lincke et al. (2021)

Role clarity	Workers' clarity of understanding of their work role in terms of task content, expectations, and responsibilities	"Do you know exactly what is expected of you at work?" (3)	5-point scale (1 = *to a small extent*, 5 = *to a great extent*)	0.83	Burr et al. (2019); Lincke et al. (2021)
Quality of leadership	Leadership quality of the next higher supervisor's behavior	"To what extent would you say that your immediate superior is good at work planning?" (4)	5-point scale (1 = *to a small extent*, 5 = *to a great extent*)	0.91	Burr et al. (2019); Lincke et al. (2021)
Support at work	Perceived availability of social support from colleagues and supervisors if needed	"How often do you get help and support from your colleagues, if needed?" (4)	5-point scale (1 = *never*, 5 = *always*)	0.86	Burr et al. (2019); Lincke et al. (2021)
Feedback	Availability of feedback from coworkers and supervisors regarding the quality of one's work	"How often does your immediate superior talk with you about how well you carry out your work?" (2)	5-point scale (1 = *never*, 5 = *always*)	0.73	Burr et al. (2019); Lincke et al. (2021)
Quantity of social relations	Possibility to interact with others during work hours	"Is it possible for you to talk to your colleagues while you are working?"	5-point scale (1 = *never*, 5 = *always*)	–	Burr et al. (2019); Lincke et al. (2021)
Sense of community	Extent to which workers feel that they are part of the group of employees at the workplace	"Is there a good atmosphere between you and your colleagues?" (2)	5-point scale (1 = *never*, 5 = *always*)	0.88	Burr et al. (2019); Lincke et al. (2021)
Trust and justice	Extent to which workers trust their management and others at work regarding task distribution and the handling of conflicts and suggestions	"Does the management trust the employees to do their work well?" (4)	5-point scale (1 = *to a small extent*, 5 = *to a great extent*)	0.85	Burr et al. (2019); Lincke et al. (2021)
Recognition	Extent to which workers feel recognized and appreciated by the management for their effort at work	"Is your work recognized and appreciated by the management?"	5-point scale (1 = *to a small extent*, 5 = *to a great extent*)	–	Burr et al. (2019); Lincke et al. (2021)

constitute "too much of a good thing" (Rudolph & Zacher, 2024). Moreover, in the months following the COVID-19 pandemic, which started in March 2020 and was officially declared over in May 2023 by the World Health Organization, many organizations tried to bring workers back to the office, and working from home may have lost some of its attraction for workers.

Work meaningfulness was weakly positively related to job level and income, whereas all other associations were non-significant. Thus, the weak positive association between work hours and work meaningfulness found by Zacher and Baumeister (2024) was not replicated in the study conducted for this book.

Finally, work psychological richness was weakly positively related to job tenure, job level, supervisory status, work hours, and shift work. Thus, Zacher and Baumeister's (2024) findings regarding positive associations between job level and both job satisfaction and work psychological richness were replicated in the current study. In contrast, the positive association between financial difficulties and work psychological richness was not replicated.

The non-significant associations between the dummy-coded (i.e., binary) industry variable and the three dimensions of the good working life are shown in Table 5.2. Notwithstanding, I explored differences between the 21 industry categories according to the Statistical Classification of Economic Activities in the European Community, which is commonly referred to as NACE (for the French term "nomenclature statistique des activités économiques dans la Communauté européenne"). Figure 5.1 shows how workers were distributed across industries, ranging from ten participants in industry category B (mining and quarrying) to 265 workers in industry category O (public administration and defense; compulsory social security). Analyses of variance showed that there were statistically significant differences between industries for each of the three dimensions of the good working life (controlled for the respective other two dimensions).

Using standardized scores (i.e., mean of zero), Fig. 5.1 displays profiles of the good working life for each of the 21 industries represented in the study conducted for this book. Table 5.3 presents rankings of industries for each of the three dimensions of the good working life, ranging from highest to lowest average scores (always controlled for the respective other two dimensions of the good working life). Regarding job satisfaction, the

Table 5.2 Partial correlations between employment characteristics and dimensions of the good working life (corrected for the respective other two dimensions of the good working life)

	Job satisfaction	*Work meaningfulness*	*Work psychological richness*
Job tenure	(−0.002)	(−0.03)	0.05
Job level	0.06	0.05	0.09
Income	(−0.01)	0.07	(0.04)
Financial difficulties	−0.17	(−0.01)	(0.02)
Industry (1 = primary/secondary, 2 = tertiary)	(0.001)	(0.02)	(0.03)
Supervisory status (1 = no, 2 = yes)	(0.04)	(0.04)	0.08
Work hours	−0.06	(−0.02)	0.06
Shift work (1 = day, 2 = shift)	−0.09	(−0.02)	0.09
Contract type (1 = permanent, 2 = temporary)	(−0.03)	(0.01)	(−0.01)
Working from home (% of time)	(−0.02)	(0.03)	(−0.03)

Note: N = Due to missing data, N ranged from 2115 to 2050. Non-significant correlations ($p > 0.05$) are shown in parentheses

three industries with the highest average scores were R (arts, entertainment, and recreation), I (accommodation and food service activities), and L (real estate activities), whereas the three industries with the lowest average scores were Q (human health and social work activities), U (activities of extraterritorial organizations and bodies), and B (mining and quarrying). Regarding work meaningfulness, the three industries with the highest average scores were E (water supply; sewerage, waste management, and remediation activities), M (professional, scientific, and technical activities), and P (education), whereas the three lowest scoring industries were B (mining and quarrying), R (arts, entertainment, and recreation), and I (accommodation and food service activities). Finally, regarding work psychological richness, the three industries with the highest average scores were I (accommodation and good service activities), B (mining and quarrying), and Q (human health and social work activities), whereas the three industries with the lowest average scores on this dimension were T (activities of households as employers; undifferentiated goods and services producing activities of households for own use), E (water supply; sewerage,

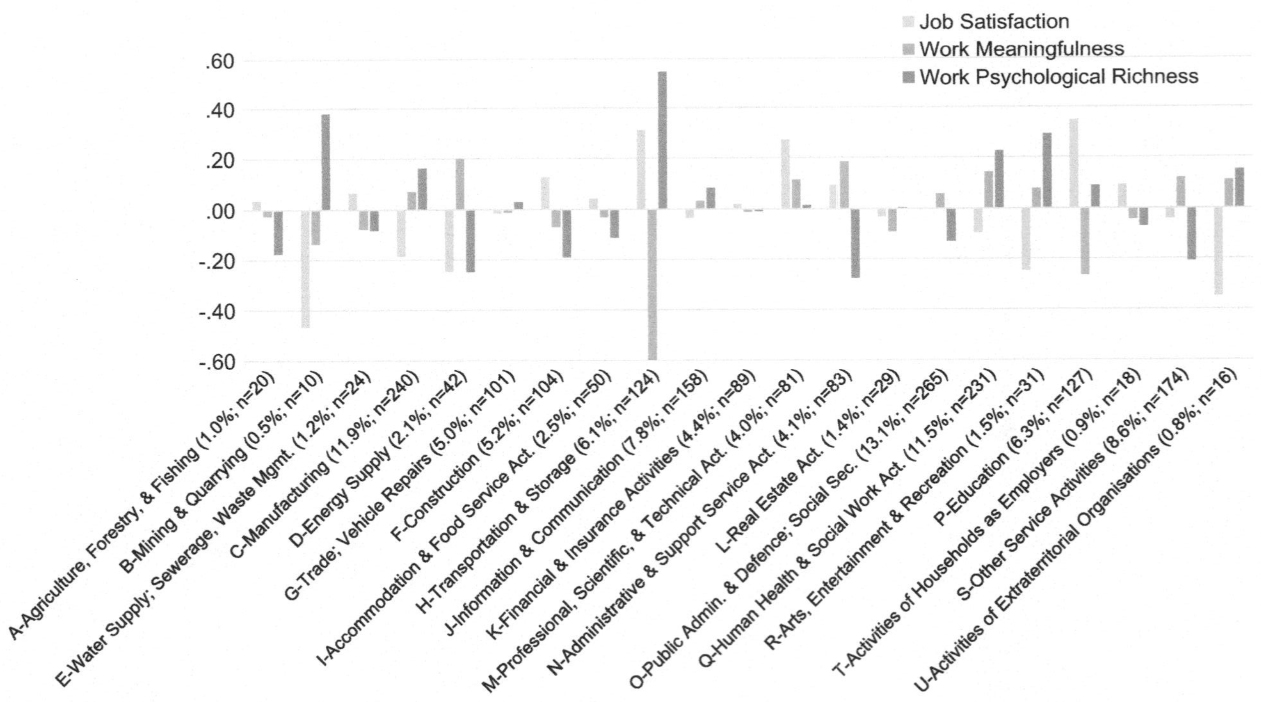

Fig. 5.1 Standardized industry differences in dimensions of the good working life (controlling for the respective other two dimensions)

Table 5.3 Ranking of industries regarding the dimensions of the good working life (controlled for the respective other two dimensions)

Rank (1 = highest to 21 = lowest)	*Job satisfaction*	*Work meaningfulness*	*Work psychological richness*
1	R—arts, entertainment and recreation	E—water supply; sewerage, waste management and remediation activities	I—accommodation and food service activities
2	I—accommodation and food service activities	M—professional, scientific and technical activities	B—mining and quarrying
3	L—real estate activities	P—education	Q—human health and social work activities
4	G—wholesale and retail trade; repair of motor vehicles and motorcycles	T—activities of households as employers; undifferentiated goods and services producing activities of households for own use	P—education
5	M—professional, scientific, and technical activities	L—real estate activities	D—electricity, gas, steam, and air conditioning supply
6	S—other service activities	U—activities of extraterritorial organizations and bodies	U—activities of extraterritorial organizations and bodies
7	C—manufacturing	Q—human health and social work activities	R—arts, entertainment and recreation
8	H—transportation and storage	D—electricity, gas, steam, and air conditioning supply	J—information and communication
9	A—agriculture, forestry and fishing	O—public administration and defense; compulsory social security	F—construction

(*continued*)

Table 5.3 (continued)

Rank (1 = highest to 21 = lowest)	*Job satisfaction*	*Work meaningfulness*	*Work psychological richness*
10	K—financial and insurance activities	J—information and communication	L—real estate activities
11	O—public administration and defense; compulsory social security	K—financial and insurance activities	N—administrative and support service activities
12	F—construction	F—construction	K—financial and insurance activities
13	N—administrative and support service activities	A—agriculture, forestry, and fishing	S—other service activities
14	J—information and communication	H—transportation and storage	C—manufacturing
15	T—activities of households as employers; undifferentiated goods and services producing activities of households for own use	S—other service activities	H—transportation and storage
16	P—education	G—wholesale and retail trade; repair of motor vehicles and motorcycles	O—public administration and defense; compulsory social security
17	D—electricity, gas, steam and air conditioning supply	C—manufacturing	A—agriculture, forestry and fishing
18	E—water supply; sewerage, waste management and remediation activities	N—administrative and support service activities	G—wholesale and retail trade; repair of motor vehicles and motorcycles
19	Q—human health and social work activities	B—mining and quarrying	T—activities of households as employers; undifferentiated goods and services producing activities of households for own use

(*continued*)

Table 5.3 (continued)

Rank (1 = highest to 21 = lowest)	*Job satisfaction*	*Work meaningfulness*	*Work psychological richness*
20	U—activities of extraterritorial organizations and bodies	R—arts, entertainment and recreation	E—water supply; sewerage, waste management and remediation activities
21	B—mining and quarrying	I—accommodation and food service activities	M—professional, scientific and technical activities

waste management, and remediation activities), and M (professional, scientific, and technical activities).

Overall, these findings suggest that industries that score particularly high on one dimension of the good working life may be more likely to score rather low on one or both of the other two dimensions of the good working life. For example, people working in industry Q (human health and social work activities) score low on job satisfaction, high on work psychological richness, and slightly above average on work meaningfulness (rank 7 in Table 5.3). However, when interpreting the findings on industry differences, the relatively small number of participants in some industry categories should be taken into account.

Job Stressors

In the first study on the good working life, Zacher and Baumeister (2024) explored partial correlations between various job characteristics and job satisfaction, work meaningfulness, and work psychological richness. They found that key job stressors, including workload, interruptions, environmental stressors, social undermining (by supervisors and coworkers), and job insecurity, were generally negatively related to job satisfaction but generally positively related to work psychological richness. Two of these job stressors were also weakly positively related to work meaningfulness (i.e., qualitative and quantitative workload), whereas the other job stressors were not significantly associated with work meaningfulness.

In the new study conducted for this book, I measured job characteristics with the third version of the Copenhagen Psychosocial Questionnaire (COPSOQ), a reliable, well-validated, and internationally widely used instrument to assess important job stressors and job resources (Burr et al., 2019; Lincke et al., 2021). The ten job stressors included in this instrument are quantitative demands, emotional demands, hiding emotions, work privacy conflicts, dissolution, role conflicts, unfair treatment, work environment/physical demands, job insecurity, and insecurity over working conditions (see Table 5.1 for definitions, example items, response formats, reliability estimates, and sources of the measures). Table 5.4 presents the results of the partial correlation analyses for the job stressors and the three dimensions of the good working life. The table also includes a column in which the current findings are compared with the findings of the study by Zacher and Baumeister (2024). The findings on job stressors are also graphically summarized in Fig. 5.2.

All of the job stressors were moderately to strongly negatively related to job satisfaction. The strongest negative partial correlations emerged for work privacy conflicts, role conflicts, and insecurity over working conditions. In contrast, most of the job stressors, with the exceptions of job insecurity and insecurity over working conditions, were weakly to moderately positively related to work psychological richness. The strongest positive correlations emerged for emotional demands, hiding emotions, as well as dissolution and role conflicts. Additionally, the job stressors were mostly non-significantly related to work meaningfulness; an exception is dissolution, which was very weakly positively related to work meaningfulness. Thus, job stressors are detrimental to job satisfaction but do not generally affect work meaningfulness. Moreover, many job stressors seem to contribute to a more interesting, psychologically rich working life. Overall, these findings replicate the previous findings on job stressors and the good working life by Zacher and Baumeister (2024). They also extend their work by considering six additional job stressors (e.g., emotional demands, work privacy conflicts, role conflicts, and insecurity over working conditions; see Table 5.4).

Table 5.4 Partial correlations between job characteristics and dimensions of the good working life (corrected for the respective other two dimensions of the good working life)

	Job satisfaction	*Work meaningfulness*	*Work psychological richness*	*Do the findings replicate the findings of Zacher and Baumeister (2024)?*
Job stressors				
Quantitative demands	−0.28	(0.02)	0.17	Yes, for job satisfaction and work psychological richness. Zacher and Baumeister (2024) also found a weak positive relation between quantitative demands and work meaningfulness.
Emotional demands	−0.30	(0.03)	0.35	Not investigated.
Hiding emotions	−0.30	(−0.04)	0.21	Not investigated.
Work privacy conflicts	−0.43	(0.02)	0.16	Not investigated.
Dissolution	−0.19	0.05	0.18	Not investigated.
Role conflicts	−0.35	(−0.04)	0.18	Not investigated.
Unfair treatment	−0.28	(0.03)	0.10	Yes, Zacher and Baumeister (2024) found similar relations for supervisor and coworker undermining.
Work environment/ physical demands	−0.26	(0.02)	0.12	Yes.
Job insecurity	−0.24	(−0.02)	(0.03)	Yes, for job satisfaction and work meaningfulness. Zacher and Baumeister (2024) also found a weak positive relation between job insecurity and work psychological richness.
Insecurity over working conditions	−0.32	(0.04)	(0.03)	Not investigated.

(*continued*)

Table 5.4 (continued)

	Job satisfaction	*Work meaningfulness*	*Work psychological richness*	*Do the findings replicate the findings of Zacher and Baumeister (2024)?*
Job resources				
Influence at work	0.12	0.10	0.15	Yes, for job satisfaction and work psychological richness. Zacher and Baumeister (2024) did not find a significant relation between job autonomy and work meaningfulness.
Degrees of freedom (breaks/ holidays)	0.24	(−0.04)	(0.01)	Not investigated.
Possibilities for development	0.21	0.12	0.37	Yes.
Predictability of work	0.29	0.13	0.09	Not investigated.
Role clarity	0.27	0.08	0.11	Not investigated.
Quality of leadership	0.24	0.16	0.09	Yes, for supervisor support.
Support at work	0.27	(0.04)	0.12	Yes, for job satisfaction and work psychological richness. Zacher and Baumeister (2024) also found weak positive relations between supervisor and coworker support and work meaningfulness.
Feedback	0.08	0.13	0.15	Not investigated.
Quantity of social relations	0.14	(−0.03)	0.09	Not investigated.
Sense of community	0.27	(−0.02)	0.10	Not investigated.
Trust and justice	0.34	0.12	0.08	Not investigated.
Recognition	0.26	0.14	0.09	Not investigated.

Note: N = Due to missing data, N ranged from 2115 to 2050. Zacher and Baumeister (2024) additionally investigated qualitative workload and work interruptions as job stressors, as well as skill variety, perceived contribution (task identity), participation, and perceived organizational support as job resources, which were not considered in the current study. Non-significant correlations ($p > 0.05$) are shown in parentheses

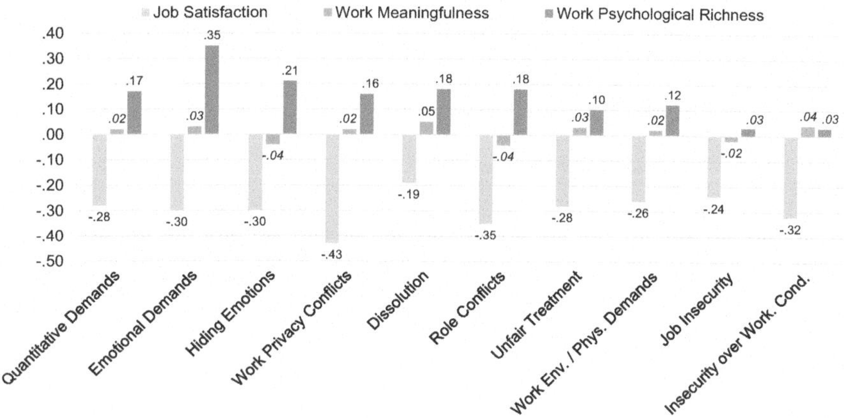

Fig. 5.2 Partial correlations between job stressors and dimensions of the good working life

Job Resources

In the initial study on the good working life, Zacher and Baumeister (2024) investigated eight job resources: job autonomy, skill variety, perceived contribution, participation, development opportunities, as well as workplace social support provided by supervisors, coworkers, and the organization. These job resources were generally positively related to both job satisfaction and work psychological richness. Most of these job resources were also weakly positively related to work meaningfulness, with the exceptions of job autonomy, skill variety, and perceived organizational support.

In the new study conducted for this book, I measured 12 task-related and social job resources with the COPSOQ instrument (Burr et al., 2019; Lincke et al., 2021): influence at work, degrees of freedom (e.g., regarding work breaks), possibilities for development, predictability of work, role clarity, quality of leadership, support at work, feedback, quantity of social relations, sense of community, trust and justice, and recognition (see Table 5.1 for definitions, example items, response formats, reliability estimates, and sources of the measures). The results of the partial correlation analyses for the job resources and the three dimensions of the good working life are shown in Table 5.4, and Fig. 5.3 graphically depicts these findings.

Fig. 5.3 Partial correlations between job resources and dimensions of the good working life

All of the job resources were weakly to moderately positively related to job satisfaction. The strongest correlations emerged for trust and justice, predictability of work, role clarity, support at work, and sense of community. With the exceptions of degrees of freedom, support at work, quantity of social relations, and sense of community, the job resources were also weakly positively related to work meaningfulness. The strongest positive correlations emerged for quality of leadership, recognition, predictability of work, and feedback. The job resources were also weakly positively related to work psychological richness, with the exception of degrees of freedom. The strongest positive correlations were found for possibilities for development, influence at work, and feedback.

Overall, these findings suggest that the vast majority of job resources have beneficial effects on the good working life, especially for job satisfaction, but also to some extent for work meaningfulness and work psychological richness. The current findings largely replicate the previous findings on job resources and the good working life by Zacher and Baumeister (2024), who also found consistent and positive associations between job resources and job satisfaction and work psychological richness, but also several positive associations between job resources and work meaningfulness. Importantly, the findings of the current study extend the initial study by Zacher and Baumeister (2024) by considering six additional job stressors (e.g., role clarity, feedback, trust and justice, and recognition; see Table 5.4).

Summary

The results presented in this chapter suggest that workers' employment characteristics, such as tenure, job level, income, supervisory status, work hours, and contract type, are generally only weakly or not significantly related to the three dimensions of the good working life. However, there were significant differences in profiles of the good working life across the 21 industries in which study participants worked. For example, for workers employed in the industry, "human health and social work," average job satisfaction was relatively low, whereas work psychological richness was relatively high, and work meaningfulness was slightly above average. In contrast, workers in the industry of "arts, entertainment, and recreation" reported relatively high job satisfaction and above-average work psychological richness, but relatively low levels of work meaningfulness. Finally, replicating and extending previous research on job characteristics and the good working life (Zacher & Baumeister, 2024), key job stressors were generally negatively related to job satisfaction, positively related to work psychological richness, and not significantly related to work meaningfulness. In contrast, key job resources were generally positively related to all three dimensions of the good working life.

References

Burr, H., Berthelsen, H., Moncada, S., Nübling, M., Dupret, E., Demiral, Y., et al. (2019). The third version of the Copenhagen psychosocial questionnaire. *Safety and Health at Work, 10*(4), 482–503. https://doi.org/10.1016/j.shaw.2019.10.002

Caleyachetty, A., Lewis, S., McNeill, A., & Leonardi-Bee, J. (2012). Struggling to make ends meet: Exploring pathways to understand why smokers in financial difficulties are less likely to quit successfully. *The European Journal of Public Health, 22*, 41–48. https://doi.org/10.1093/eurpub/ckr199

Eurostat. (2008). *NACE Rev. 2: Statistical classification of economic activities in the European community*. European Commission. https://ec.europa.eu/eurostat/documents/3859598/5902521/KS-RA-07-015-EN.PDF

Lincke, H. J., Vomstein, M., Lindner, A., Nolle, I., Häberle, N., Haug, A., & Nübling, M. (2021). COPSOQ III in Germany: Validation of a standard instrument to measure psychosocial factors at work. *Journal of Occupational Medicine and Toxicology, 16*, 1–15. https://doi.org/10.1186/s12995-021-00331-1

Rudolph, C. W., & Zacher, H. (2024). Working from home: When is it too much of a good thing? *Human Resource Development Quarterly.* https://doi.org/10.1002/hrdq.21530

von Hippel, C., Kalokerinos, E. K., & Henry, J. D. (2013). Stereotype threat among older employees: Relationships with job attitudes and turnover intentions. *Psychology and Aging, 28*(1), 17–27. https://doi.org/10.1037/a0029825

Zacher, H., & Baumeister, R. F. (2024). Differences among a satisfied, a meaningful, and a psychologically rich working life. *Journal of Positive Psychology.* https://doi.org/10.1080/17439760.2024.2417102

CHAPTER 6

The Good Working Life and Work Outcomes

Abstract In this chapter, I examine relations between the three dimensions of the good working life—job satisfaction, work meaningfulness, and work psychological richness—and several key work outcomes, including job engagement, work performance, job fatigue, and turnover intentions. Job satisfaction was generally positively related to favorable work outcomes and negatively related to job fatigue and turnover intentions. Work meaningfulness and work psychological richness were generally only weakly or non-significantly related to favorable work outcomes. Exceptions were job engagement, which was moderately and positively related to all three dimensions of the good working life, and job proactivity, which positively related to work meaningfulness and psychological richness (but not job satisfaction). Finally, work psychological richness was positively related to job fatigue, suggesting that interesting, emotionally intense, and perspective-changing work experiences may be exhausting for workers.

Keywords Job engagement • Work performance • Job proactivity • Job fatigue • Turnover intentions

The goal of this chapter is to examine unique and differential associations between the three dimensions of the good working life—job satisfaction, work meaningfulness, and work psychological richness—and several key

H. Zacher, *The Good Working Life*,
https://doi.org/10.1007/978-3-031-77221-4_6

work outcomes, including job engagement, work performance (including job proficiency, adaptivity, proactivity, career performance, team performance, innovative performance, and organizational performance; Griffin et al., 2007; Welbourne et al., 1998), as well as job fatigue (Frone & Tidwell, 2015) and turnover intentions (Adams & Beehr, 1998; Holtom et al., 2008). The definitions and operationalizations (including example items and response scales) of these work outcomes are summarized in Table 6.1.

In the first study on the good working life, Zacher and Baumeister (2024) also explored relations between the three dimensions of the good working life and several work outcomes. They found that job satisfaction was uniquely and positively related to job proficiency, job engagement, work ability, and work-family balance. In contrast, job satisfaction was negatively related to job fatigue, turnover intentions, as well as sickness absenteeism and presenteeism. Job satisfaction was not significantly related to job adaptivity and was negatively related to job proactivity. Work meaningfulness was also related to several of these outcomes, such that workers who experienced their work as meaningful reported higher job proficiency, adaptivity, proactivity, job engagement, and work-family balance, as well as lower turnover intentions and sickness absenteeism. Finally, work psychological richness was uniquely and positively related to job adaptivity, job proactivity, and job engagement but was not significantly related to job proficiency. Work psychological richness was positively related to job fatigue, turnover intentions, and sickness presenteeism, suggesting a "dark side" of interesting and complex work.

In the new study conducted for this book, I measured similar work outcomes to those explored by Zacher and Baumeister (2024), including job engagement, job proficiency, adaptivity, and proactivity, as well as job fatigue and turnover intentions. I extend this earlier study by additionally measuring workers' ratings of how their supervisor would rate their career, innovation, team, and organizational performance using a reliable, validated, and widely used role-based performance scale (Welbourne et al., 1998). Table 6.2 presents the results of the partial correlation analyses for the favorable and unfavorable work outcomes. The table also includes a column in which the findings of the study conducted for this book are compared with the findings of the initial study by Zacher and Baumeister (2024). Moreover, the findings on the work performance correlates are graphically summarized in Fig. 6.1.

Table 6.1 Work outcomes: definitions and operationalizations

Construct	*Definition*	*Example item*	*Response format*	*Cronbach's alpha*	*Source*
Job engagement	The investment of cognitive, affective, and physical energies into the work role	"At work, I focus a great deal of attention on my job." (9)	7-point Likert scale (1 = *strongly disagree*, 7 = *strongly agree*)	0.92	Rich et al. (2010)
Job proficiency	Extent to which one meets the expectations and requirements of the work role	"I carry out the core parts of my job well." (3)	7-point scale (1 = *never*, 7 = *always*)	0.84	Griffin et al. (2007)
Job adaptivity	Extent to which one copes with, responds to, and supports changes that impact the work role	"I adapt well to changes in my core tasks." (3)	7-point scale (1 = *never*, 7 = *always*)	0.85	Griffin et al. (2007)
Job proactivity	Extent to which one engages in self-starting, future-oriented behavior to change work roles and situations	"I initiate better ways of doing my core tasks." (3)	7-point scale (1 = *never*, 7 = *always*)	0.87	Griffin et al. (2007)
Career performance	Extent to which one obtains the necessary skills to progress through one's organization	"Seeking out career opportunities." (4)	5-point scale (1 = *needs much improvement*, 7 = *excellent*)	0.90	Welbourne et al. (1998)

(*continued*)

Table 6.1 (continued)

Construct	*Definition*	*Example item*	*Response format*	*Cronbach's alpha*	*Source*
Innovation performance	Extent to which one shows creativity and innovation in one's job and the organization	"Finding improved ways to do things." (4)	5-point scale (1 = *needs much improvement*, 7 = *excellent*)	0.90	Welbourne et al. (1998)
Team performance	Extent to which one works with coworkers toward the success of the organizations	"Working as part of a team or work group." (4)	5-point scale (1 = *needs much improvement*, 7 = *excellent*)	0.91	Welbourne et al. (1998)
Organizational performance	Extent to which one goes above the call of duty in one's concern for the organization	"Helping so that the company is a good place to be." (4)	5-point scale (1 = *needs much improvement*, 7 = *excellent*)	0.89	Welbourne et al. (1998)
Job fatigue	Extreme tiredness and reduced functional capacity experienced during and at the end of the workday	"How often do you feel physically drained at the end of the work day?" (9)	7-point scale (1 = *never*, 7 = *always*)	0.95	Frone and Tidwell (2015)
Turnover intentions	Willingness or intention to voluntarily quit one's job or leave an organization	"I am planning to leave my job for another in the near future." (3)	7-point Likert scale (1 = *strongly disagree*, 7 = *strongly agree*)	0.95	Adams and Beehr (1998)

Table 6.2 Partial correlations between dimensions of the good working life and work Outcomes (Corrected for the Respective Other Two Dimensions of the Good Working Life)

	Job satisfaction	*Work meaningfulness*	*Work psychological richness*	*Do the findings replicate the findings of Zacher and Baumeister (2024)?*
Job engagement	0.34	0.18	0.32	Yes.
Job proficiency[a]	0.22	(−0.004)	0.10	Only for job satisfaction. Zacher and Baumeister (2024) found a positive association between work meaningfulness and job proficiency, and no significant association between work psychological richness and job proficiency.
Job adaptivity[a]	0.21	(0.04)	0.15	Only for work psychological richness. Zacher and Baumeister (2024) found no significant association between job adaptivity and job satisfaction and a positive association between work meaningfulness and job adaptivity.
Job proactivity[a]	(−0.01)	0.15	0.19	Yes, for work meaningfulness and work psychological richness. Zacher and Baumeister (2024) also found a negative relation between job proactivity and job satisfaction.
Career performance[a]	0.21	0.08	0.17	Not investigated.
Innovation performance[a]	0.21	0.10	0.16	Not investigated.
Team performance[a]	0.26	(0.01)	0.15	Not investigated.
Organizational performance[a]	0.26	0.06	0.13	Not investigated.
Job fatigue	−0.48	(−0.02)	0.14	Yes.
Turnover intentions	−0.52	−0.06	(0.04)	Yes, for job satisfaction and work meaningfulness. Zacher and Baumeister (2024) also found a positive relation between work psychological richness and turnover intentions.

Note: $N = 2280$

[a] $N = 1326$ (assessed at Time 2). Non-significant correlations ($p > 0.05$) are shown in parentheses

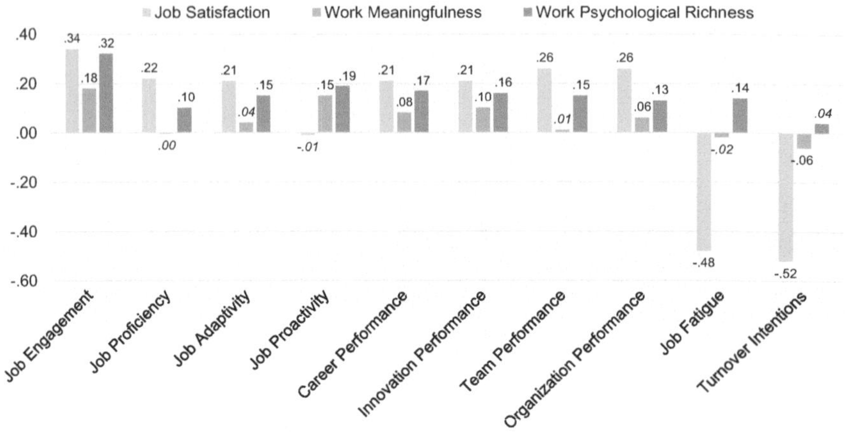

Fig. 6.1 Partial correlations between dimensions of the good working life and work outcomes

Job Engagement and Performance

Job engagement involves workers' investment of physical, emotional, and cognitive energy into the work role (Rich et al., 2010). For example, engaged workers are more likely to show effort, enthusiasm, and absorption at work compared to disengaged workers. All three dimensions of the good working life were uniquely and positively associated with job engagement. These findings replicate earlier findings by Zacher and Baumeister (2024), suggesting that investing high levels of physical, emotional, and cognitive energy into one's work role generally contributes to a good working life (and vice versa). According to Griffin et al. (2007), job proficiency refers to the extent to which workers meet the formal expectations and requirements of their work role (also called task performance). Job adaptivity entails the extent to which workers cope with, respond to, and support changes that impact their work role. Finally, job proactivity describes the extent to which workers engage in self-starting, future-oriented behavior to change work roles and situations (also called personal initiative or proactive work behavior; Griffin et al., 2007). The findings for work performance only partially replicated Zacher and Baumeister's (2024) earlier findings (see Table 6.2). The current study found a positive relation between job satisfaction and job proficiency, which is also consistent with previous meta-analytic work (Judge et al., 2001; Riketta, 2008). In contrast, job proficiency was not significantly related to work meaningfulness and only weakly positively related to work psychological richness. As in Zacher and Baumeister (2024), job adaptivity was positively related to work psychological richness but also positively related to job satisfaction. In contrast, the relation between job adaptivity and work meaningfulness was not significant. Similar to Zacher and Baumeister (2024), job proactivity was positively related to work meaningfulness and work psychological richness in the current study. In contrast, there was a nonsignificant relation between job proactivity and job satisfaction, and thus, the negative relation between these constructs found by Zacher and Baumeister (2024) was not replicated in the current study.

Workers' career, innovation, team, and organizational performance were not examined in previous research on the good working life. According to Welbourne et al. (1998), career performance involves the extent to which workers obtain the skills needed to progress through their organization, such as seeking out career opportunities. Innovation performance refers to the extent to which workers show creativity and innovation-related efforts in their job and organization, such as inventing new products or finding improved ways to do things. Team performance entails the extent to which workers collaborate with their coworkers toward the success of the team and their organization. Finally, organizational performance (also called organizational citizenship behavior) involves the extent to which workers do above and beyond the call of duty in their concerns for their organization and its members. For example, workers with high levels of organizational performance are more likely to help out and make the organization a better place to be through their behavior at work (Welbourne et al., 1998).

The four work-role performance dimensions were all moderately and positively related to job satisfaction and—somewhat more weakly and positively—to work psychological richness. The relations between these performance dimensions and work meaningfulness were also, with the exception of team performance, positive, albeit very weak. Overall, these findings suggest that workers who show high levels of performance in terms of their careers, innovation, team membership, and organizational citizenship are more likely to experience a good working life.

Job Fatigue and Turnover Intentions

Job fatigue involves extreme levels of tiredness and reduced functional capacity experienced during and at the end of the work day. It involved feeling physically, emotionally, and cognitively exhausted and drained due to one's work (Frone & Tidwell, 2015). Turnover intentions refer to workers' willingness or intention to voluntarily quit their jobs and leave their organizations (Adams & Beehr, 1998; Holtom et al., 2008). Similar to the initial findings of Zacher and Baumeister (2024), job satisfaction was strongly and negatively related to both job fatigue and turnover intentions (see Table 6.2). In contrast, work meaningfulness was only weakly or non-significantly related to these unfavorable work outcomes. The current study also replicated the positive relation between work psychological richness and job fatigue found by Zacher and Baumeister (2024), whereas no significant association was found between turnover intentions and this dimension of the good working life. These findings suggest that job satisfaction may protect, whereas work psychological richness may enhance workers' job fatigue. Moreover, satisfied workers also seem less likely to quit their job.

Summary

The three dimensions of the good working life were uniquely and differentially associated with several important work outcomes. All three dimensions seem to contribute positively to job engagement, whereas only job satisfaction and—to a lesser extent—work psychological richness benefit job proficiency, job adaptivity, as well as career, innovation, team, and organizational performance. Job proactivity stands out here, as it was unrelated to job satisfaction but moderately and positively related to both work meaningfulness and psychological richness. Finally, as already shown in previous research, job satisfaction was negatively associated with both job fatigue and turnover intentions, whereas work psychological richness was positively related to job fatigue. Overall, these findings suggest that, generally, job satisfaction contributes to favorable work outcomes and helps prevent negative work outcomes, whereas work psychological richness may lead to both favorable and certain negative outcomes, particularly job fatigue. Finally, compared to job satisfaction and work psychological richness, work meaningfulness seems to play only a subordinate role in the work outcomes investigated.

References

Adams, G. A., & Beehr, T. A. (1998). Turnover and retirement: A comparison of their similarities and differences. *Personnel Psychology, 51*(3), 643–665. https://doi.org/10.1111/j.1744-6570.1998.tb00255.x

Frone, M. R., & Tidwell, M. C. O. (2015). The meaning and measurement of work fatigue: Development and evaluation of the three-dimensional work fatigue inventory (3D-WFI). *Journal of Occupational Health Psychology, 20*(3), 273–288. https://doi.org/10.1037/a0038700

Griffin, M. A., Neal, A., & Parker, S. K. (2007). A new model of work role performance: Positive behavior in uncertain and interdependent contexts. *Academy of Management Journal, 50*, 327–347. https://doi.org/10.5465/AMJ.2007.24634438

Holtom, B. C., Mitchell, T. R., Lee, T. W., & Eberly, M. B. (2008). Turnover and retention research: A glance at the past, a closer review of the present, and a venture into the future. *Academy of Management Annals, 2*(1), 231–274. https://doi.org/10.1080/19416520802211552

Judge, T. A., Thorensen, C. J., Bono, J. E., & Patton, G. K. (2001). The job satisfaction-job performance relationship: A qualitative and quantitative review. *Psychological Bulletin, 127*(3), 376–407. https://doi.org/10.1037/0033-2909.127.3.376

Rich, B. L., LePine, J. A., & Crawford, E. A. (2010). Job engagement: Antecedents and effects on job performance. *Academy of Management Journal, 53*(3), 617–635. https://doi.org/10.5465/AMJ.2010.51468988

Riketta, M. (2008). The causal relation between job attitudes and performance: A meta-analysis of panel studies. *Journal of Applied Psychology, 93*(2), 472–481. https://doi.org/10.1037/0021-9010.93.2.472

Welbourne, T. M., Johnson, D. E., & Erez, A. (1998). The role-based performance scale: Validity analysis of a theory-based measure. *Academy of Management Journal, 41*(5), 540–555. https://doi.org/10.2307/256941

Zacher, H., & Baumeister, R. F. (2024). Differences among a satisfied, a meaningful, and a psychologically rich working life. *Journal of Positive Psychology.* https://doi.org/10.1080/17439760.2024.2417102

CHAPTER 7

The Good Working Life and Life Outcomes

Abstract In this chapter, I examine relations between the three dimensions of the good working life—job satisfaction, work meaningfulness, and work psychological richness—and several important life outcomes, including life satisfaction, meaning in life, psychological richness in general, physical and mental health, generativity, and wisdom. All three dimensions of the good working life were uniquely and positively related to life satisfaction. Job satisfaction was negatively related to meaning in life, whereas work meaningfulness was strongly positively related to meaning in life. Work psychological richness was strongly positively related to psychological richness in life in general, whereas job satisfaction and work meaningfulness had only weak effects. Job satisfaction, but not work meaningfulness and psychological richness, positively related to physical and mental health and wisdom. In contrast, work meaningfulness and work psychological richness, but not job satisfaction, positively predicted generativity.

Keywords Life satisfaction • Meaning in life • Physical health • Mental health • Generativity • Wisdom

The goal of this chapter is to examine unique and differential associations between the three dimensions of the good working life—job satisfaction, work meaningfulness, and work psychological richness—and several

H. Zacher, *The Good Working Life*,
https://doi.org/10.1007/978-3-031-77221-4_7

important life outcomes, including life satisfaction, meaning in life, and psychological richness in life (i.e., three dimensions representing "the good life" in general). Additionally, I explore relations between the three dimensions of the good working life and physical and mental health, generativity, and wisdom. The definitions and operationalizations of these important life outcomes are summarized in Table 7.1.

In their initial study on the good working life, Zacher and Baumeister (2024) examined partial correlations between the three dimensions of the good working life and life satisfaction, family satisfaction, as well as physical and mental health. They found relatively strong positive correlations between job satisfaction and all of these more general well-being outcomes. Additionally, they found weak positive correlations between work meaningfulness and family and life satisfaction (but no significant relations with physical and mental health) and weak negative correlations between work psychological richness and physical and mental health (but no significant relations with family and life satisfaction). In the new study conducted for this book, I aimed to replicate and extend these previous findings by exploring not only associations with life satisfaction and health but also with meaning in life, psychological richness in life, as well as generativity and wisdom.

Life satisfaction refers to the degree to which people positively evaluate the quality of their lives (Diener, 1984). Meaning in life involves people's belief that their life has meaning and contributes to other people and society (Peterson et al., 2005). As described in Chap. 1, psychological richness has been defined as people's experience that their life is characterized by variety, interestingness, and perspective change (Oishi & Westgate, 2022). Together, life satisfaction, meaning and life, and psychological richness can be thought of as three dimensions of the good life in general, which complement the three good working life dimensions that represent the focus of this book. Physical health refers to the condition of workers' body, taking into consideration everything from the absence of disease to physical fitness level. Likewise, mental health involves workers' condition with regard to their psychological and emotional well-being, such as the presence of symptoms of depression and anxiety (Ware et al., 1996).

The psychoanalyst Erik Erikson (1950) was the first to describe the psychosocial conflict between generativity (i.e., the concern with establishing and guiding members of future generations) and stagnation (i.e., caring only for oneself) as the seventh out of eight stages in his seminal theory of lifespan development. The virtue associated with achieving

Table 7.1 Life outcomes: definitions and operationalizations

Construct	*Definition*	*Example item*	*Response format*	*Cronbach's alpha*	*Source*
Life satisfaction	The degree to which one positively evaluates the quality of one's life	"I am satisfied with my life." (5)	7-point Likert scale (1 = *strongly disagree*, 7 = *strongly agree*)	0.90	Diener et al. (1985)
Meaning in life	The perception that one's life has meaning and contributes to other people and society	"My life serves a higher purpose." (6)	7-point Likert scale (1 = *strongly disagree*, 7 = *strongly agree*)	0.90	Peterson et al. (2005)
Psychological richness	Experiencing one's life as characterized by variety, interestingness, and perspective change	"My life is full of unique, unusual experiences." (12)	7-point Likert scale (1 = *strongly disagree*, 7 = *strongly agree*)	0.95	Oishi et al. (2019)
Physical health	The condition of one's body, taking into consideration everything from the absence of disease to fitness level	"During the past four weeks, how much of the time have you accomplished less than you would like as a result of your physical health?" (6)	3- and 5-point response scales	0.95	Ware et al. (1996)
Mental health	One's condition with regard to psychological and emotional well-being	"During the past four weeks, how much of the time have you accomplished less than you would like as a result of any emotional problems, such as feeling depressed or anxious?" (6)	3- and 5-point response scales	0.95	Ware et al. (1996)

(*continued*)

Table 7.1 (continued)

Construct	*Definition*	*Example item*	*Response format*	*Cronbach's alpha*	*Source*
Generativity	The concern for establishing and guiding the next generation	"I have made many commitments to many different kinds of people, groups, and activities in my life." (20)	5-point Likert scale (1 = *strongly disagree*, 5 = *strongly agree*)	0.85	McAdams and de St. Aubin (1992)
Wisdom	Personal characteristics with seven components: self-reflection, pro-social behaviors, emotional regulation, acceptance of diverse perspectives, decisiveness, social advising, and spirituality	"I enjoy being exposed to diverse viewpoints." (6; the item on spirituality was dropped due to a negative item-factor correlation)	5-point Likert scale (1 = *strongly disagree*, 5 = *strongly agree*)	0.65	Thomas et al. (2022)

generativity is "care." Generativity theory suggests that peoples' generative concerns may translate into a wide variety of behavioral expressions of generativity, such as teaching, mentoring, taking over leadership roles, and helping to improve the community for future generations (McAdams & de St. Aubin, 1992). Generativity in the work context is linked to higher job satisfaction, occupational well-being, and subjective career success (Ackerman et al., 2000; Clark & Arnold, 2008; Doerwald et al., 2021). The eighth and final stage of lifespan development, postulated by Erikson (1950), is integrity versus despair, which is associated with the virtue of "wisdom." Wisdom involves "the pinnacle of insight into the human condition and about the means and ends of a good life" (Baltes & Staudinger, 2000, p. 122). Recently, scholars have suggested that wisdom can be operationalized as a personal characteristic with seven interrelated components:

self-reflection, pro-social behaviors, emotional regulation, acceptance of diverse perspectives, decisiveness, social advising, and spirituality (Thomas et al., 2022). Research on wisdom in the workplace has suggested that it is associated with well-being and successful leadership (Zacher et al., 2014; Zacher et al., 2015; Zacher & Kunzmann, 2019; Zacher & Staudinger, 2018).

Table 7.2 presents the partial correlations between the three dimensions of the good working life and the various life outcomes. The table also includes a column that compares the current findings with the

Table 7.2 Partial correlations between dimensions of the good working life and life outcomes (corrected for the respective other two dimensions of the good working life)

	Job satisfaction	*Work meaningfulness*	*Work psychological richness*	*Do the findings replicate the findings of Zacher and Baumeister (2024)?*
Life satisfaction	0.21	0.12	0.16	Yes, for job satisfaction and work meaningfulness. Zacher and Baumeister (2024) did not find a significant relation between work psychological richness and life satisfaction.
Meaning in life	−0.21	0.38	0.12	Not investigated.
Psychological richness	(0.02)	0.06	0.41	Not investigated.
Physical health	0.20	(0.002)	−0.05	Yes.
Mental health	0.37	(−0.01)	(0.03)	Yes, for job satisfaction and work meaningfulness. Zacher and Baumeister (2024) also found a weak negative relation between work psychological richness and mental health.
Generativity[a]	(0.02)	0.28	0.22	Not investigated.
Wisdom[a]	0.26	(−0.05)	0.08	Not investigated.

Note: N = Due to missing data, N ranged from 2176 to 2218

[a] N = 1325 to 1326 (assessed at Time 2). Non-significant correlations ($p > 0.05$) are shown in parentheses

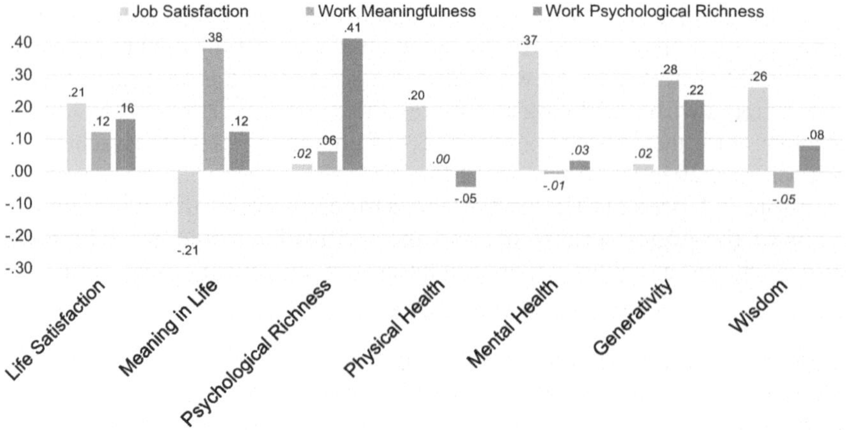

Fig. 7.1 Partial correlations between dimensions of the good working life and life outcomes

previous findings of the study by Zacher and Baumeister (2024). The unique associations between the three dimensions of the good working life and different life outcomes are also graphically summarized in Fig. 7.1.

The Good Life: Life Satisfaction, Meaning in Life, and Psychological Richness

All three dimensions of the good working life were positively related to life satisfaction, with job satisfaction being a stronger correlate than work meaningfulness and work psychological richness. This finding is consistent with research on links between job and life satisfaction, suggesting that positive experiences on the job may spill over to other life domains and contribute to satisfaction with life more broadly (Bialowolski & Weziak-Bialowolska, 2021; Judge & Watanabe, 1993). The findings for job satisfaction and work meaningfulness replicate previous findings by Zacher and Baumeister (2024). In contrast, these researchers did not find a significant association between work psychological richness and life satisfaction in their study.

Work meaningfulness was strongly and positively related to meaning in life in general, suggesting that the experience of meaningfulness at work may spill over to other life domains and contribute to a sense of meaning in life more broadly. In contrast, work psychological richness was weakly and positively related to meaning in life, and job satisfaction was even moderately and negatively related to meaning in life. It may be possible that workers who experience high levels of job satisfaction and, accordingly, invest much of their time and energy into work have less time and energy available for other meaningful pursuits in life. It may also be possible that workers who experience a general lack of meaning in life turn to their jobs as a source of personal satisfaction. Further research is necessary to elucidate this surprising result.

Finally, work psychological richness was strongly and positively related to psychological richness in life in general, suggesting that interesting and complex work experiences spill over to other life domains and contribute to a sense of a psychologically rich life more generally. In contrast, job satisfaction was not significantly related, and work meaningfulness was only very weakly and positively related to psychological richness in life in general. These findings imply that having a satisfying and meaningful job does not necessarily contribute to a psychologically rich life.

Physical and Mental Health

The findings regarding the good working life and physical and mental health largely replicated previous work by Zacher and Baumeister (2024). Job satisfaction was uniquely and positively related to both physical and mental health, with the correlation for mental health nearly twice as strong as for physical health. In contrast, work meaningfulness was not significantly related to both health dimensions, and work psychological richness was very weakly and negatively related to physical health but not significantly related to mental health. These findings suggest that workers' job satisfaction represents the only dimension of the good working life that makes an important contribution to physical and mental health, especially to mental health.

Generativity and Wisdom

The findings for generativity were the opposite as to those for physical and mental health. Specifically, job satisfaction was not significantly associated with generativity, whereas both work meaningfulness and work psychological richness had moderate and positive associations with generativity.

This suggests that meaningful and psychologically rich work can facilitate workers' perception that they are actively contributing to other people, society, and future generations.

In contrast, the findings for wisdom were more similar to those for physical and mental health. Job satisfaction was moderately and positively related to wisdom, whereas work psychological richness had a weak positive effect, and work meaningfulness did not have a significant effect on wisdom. These findings suggest that the experience of job satisfaction may be more conducive to the experience of wisdom than the experience of meaning or psychological richness at work. This finding seems to stand in contrast to assumptions by Oishi and colleagues, who argued that a psychologically rich life may represent a path to wisdom (Oishi & Westgate, 2022). Accordingly, further research on the good working life and wisdom is needed.

Summary

The three dimensions of the good working life seem to have mostly beneficial effects on broader life outcomes. Job satisfaction was positively related to life satisfaction and to physical and mental health. An odd exception was the negative relation between job satisfaction and meaning in life in general, which may be explained by workers' priorities across different life domains. Both work meaningfulness and work psychological richness were weakly to strongly positively related to all three dimensions of the good life (i.e., life satisfaction, meaning in life, psychological richness) and to generativity.

References

Ackerman, S., Zuroff, D. C., & Moskowitz, D. S. (2000). Generativity in midlife and young adults: Links to agency, communion, and subjective well-being. *International Journal of Aging and Human Development, 50*(1), 17–41. https://doi.org/10.2190/9F51-LR6T-JHRJ-2QW6

Baltes, P. B., & Staudinger, U. M. (2000). Wisdom: A metaheuristic (pragmatic) to orchastrate mind and virtue toward excellence. *American Psychologist, 55*(1), 122–136. https://doi.org/10.1037/0003-066X.55.1.122

Bialowolski, P., & Weziak-Bialowolska, D. (2021). Longitudinal evidence for reciprocal effects Between life satisfaction and job satisfaction. *Journal of Happiness Studies, 22*, 1287–1312. https://doi.org/10.1007/s10902-020-00273-1

Clark, M., & Arnold, J. (2008). The nature, prevalence and correlates of generativity among men in middle career. *Journal of Vocational Behavior, 73*(3), 473–484. https://doi.org/10.1016/j.jvb.2008.09.002

Diener, E. (1984). Subjective well-being. *Psychological Bulletin, 95*(3), 542–575. https://doi.org/10.1037/0033-2909.95.3.542

Diener, E., Emmons, R. A., Larsen, R. J., & Griffin, S. (1985). The satisfaction with life scale. *Journal of Personality Assessment, 49*(1), 71–75. https://doi.org/10.1207/s15327752jpa4901_13

Doerwald, F., Zacher, H., Scheibe, S., & van Yperen, N. W. (2021). Generativity at work: A meta-analysis. *Journal of Vocational Behavior, 125*, 103521. https://doi.org/10.1016/j.jvb.2020.103521

Erikson, E. H. (1950). *Childhood and society*. W. W. Norton.

Judge, T., & Watanabe, S. (1993). Another look at the job satisfaction-life satisfaction relationship. *Journal of Applied Psychology, 78*(6), 939–948. https://doi.org/10.1037/0021-9010.78.6.939

McAdams, D. P., & de St. Aubin, E. (1992). A theory of generativity and its assessment through self-report, behavioral acts, and narrative themes in autobiography. *Journal of Personality and Social Psychology, 62*(6), 1003–1015. https://doi.org/10.1037/0022-3514.62.6.1003

Oishi, S., Choi, H., Buttrick, N., Heintzelman, S. J., Kushlev, K., Westgate, E. C., et al. (2019). The psychologically rich life questionnaire. *Journal of Research in Personality, 81*, 257–270. https://doi.org/10.1016/j.jrp.2019.06.010

Oishi, S., & Westgate, E. C. (2022). A psychologically rich life: Beyond happiness and meaning. *Psychological Review, 129*(4), 790–811. https://doi.org/10.1037/rev0000317

Peterson, C., Park, N., & Seligman, M. E. P. (2005). Orientations to happiness and life satisfaction: The full versus the empty life. *Journal of Happiness Studies, 6*(25–41). https://doi.org/10.1007/s10902-004-1278-z

Thomas, M. L., Palmer, B. W., Lee, E. E., Liu, J., Daly, R., Tu, X. M., & Jeste, D. V. (2022). Abbreviated San Diego wisdom scale (SD-WISE-7) and Jeste-Thomas wisdom index (JTWI). *International Psychogeriatrics, 34*(7), 617–626. https://doi.org/10.1017/S1041610221002684

Ware, J. E., Kosinski, M., & Keller, S. D. (1996). A 12-item short-form health survey: Construction of scales and preliminary tests of reliability and validity. *Medical Care, 34*(3), 220–233. https://doi.org/10.1097/00005650-199603000-00003

Zacher, H., & Baumeister, R. F. (2024). Differences among a satisfied, a meaningful, and a psychologically rich working life. *Journal of Positive Psychology*. https://doi.org/10.1080/17439760.2024.2417102

Zacher, H., & Kunzmann, U. (2019). Wisdom in the workplace. In R. J. Sternberg, H. C. Nusbaum, & J. Glück (Eds.), *Applying wisdom to contemporary world problems* (pp. 255–292). Palgrave Macmillan. https://doi.org/10.1007/978-3-030-20287-3_10

Zacher, H., McKenna, B., Rooney, D., & Gold, S. (2015). Wisdom in the military context. *Military Psychology, 27*(3), 142–154. https://doi.org/10.1037/mil0000070

Zacher, H., Pearce, L. K., Rooney, D., & McKenna, B. (2014). Leaders' personal wisdom and leader-member exchange quality: The role of individualized consideration. *Journal of Business Ethics, 121*(2), 171–187. https://doi.org/10.1007/s10551-013-1692-4

Zacher, H., & Staudinger, U. M. (2018). Wisdom and well-being. In E. Diener, S. Oishi, & L. Tay (Eds.), *Handbook of well-being*. DEF. https://static1.squarespace.com/static/65f0a38858b34640d8d1d19a/t/663ba4b32297654ef513dcc0/1715184831926/Handbook-of-Well-Being.pdf

CHAPTER 8

Conclusions and Outlook

Abstract This final chapter of the book on the good working life outlines 15 key insights, limitations and suggestions for future research, as well as practical implications. The key conclusions are based on the theoretical and empirical insights regarding job satisfaction, work meaningfulness, and work psychological richness presented in the preceding chapters of this book. The suggestions for future research derive in part from the limitations of the empirical study conducted for this book and concern especially the need for further theory development and methodological improvements. The practical implications include suggestions for individual workers who want to create and maintain good working lives for themselves, leaders who aim to help workers achieve good working lives, and organizations interested in creating structural conditions under which good working lives can flourish.

Keywords The good working life • Research • Practice • Methods • Leaders • Organizations

In the preceding seven chapters, I introduced the novel concept of the good working life, including its theoretical background, dimensions, and operationalization. In a large-scale empirical study conducted for this book, including over 2000 workers from various jobs, organizations, and

H. Zacher, *The Good Working Life*,
https://doi.org/10.1007/978-3-031-77221-4_8

industries, I examined unique relations between the three dimensions of the good working life, several individual and work-related characteristics, as well as several important work and life outcomes. The findings replicate many of the results presented by Zacher and Baumeister (2024) in the first academic article on the good working life published in the *Journal of Positive Psychology*. However, the present findings also extend this previous study by including several additional individual and work-related characteristics that have so far not been investigated in relation to the good working life. In the following, I first present 15 key insights from this book. Subsequently, I address several limitations of the empirical study conducted for this book and outline suggestions for future theory development and empirical research, particularly methodological improvements. In conclusion, I provide practical implications for individual workers, leaders, and organizations regarding the good working life.

Key Insights from This Book

The theoretical considerations and empirical findings from a large-scale survey study presented in this book can be summarized in terms of 15 key insights:

1. *The good working life has three distinct dimensions*: Based on ancient philosophy and newer developments in the discipline of psychological science, the good working life can be conceptualized as consisting of three dimensions (Zacher & Baumeister, 2024). First, job satisfaction refers to a positive affective state that results from the evaluation of one's job and work-related experiences (Locke, 1976). Second, work meaningfulness involves workers' beliefs that the work they are doing is significant and important and has a positive valence in terms of personal growth and a sense of purpose (Steger et al., 2012). Third, work psychological richness entails workers' perception that their working life is characterized by complexity, entails a variety of interesting and perspective-changing experiences, and involves feeling a variety of deep emotions (see Oishi & Westgate, 2022).
2. *Half of all workers prioritize the satisfied working life*: When asked to choose only one out of three possible working lives for themselves in the empirical study conducted for this book, approximately 50% of workers chose the satisfied working life, characterized by positive emotions, joy, and happiness on the job. In contrast,

approximately one-fourth of workers prioritized the meaningful working life, which is characterized by a sense of purpose and importance related to the work one is doing. The remaining one-fourth of workers chose the psychologically rich working life, which is characterized by high levels of complexity, interesting experiences, perspective-changing experiences, and variability in feeling deep emotions. Similar results emerged when workers were asked to choose only one out of three options for their lives in general. Importantly, all three—job satisfaction, work meaningfulness, and work psychological richness—are probably important outcomes for most, if not all workers. When asked to prioritize, however, the majority of workers chose a satisfied working life. Nevertheless, substantial proportions of workers (approximately one-fourth each) gave priority preference to a meaningful or a psychologically rich working life, respectively, as opposed to a satisfied working life.

3. *The good working life can be measured*: The good working life can be measured reliably with well-validated and practical self-report questionnaires developed in psychological science (Judge et al., 1998; Oishi et al., 2019; Steger et al., 2012; Zacher & Baumeister, 2024). The average ratings of job satisfaction, work meaningfulness, and work psychological richness in the empirical study conducted for this book were somewhat higher than the midpoint of a 7-point rating scale ranging from 1 = "very low" to 7 = "very high." The average scores were somewhere between 4.5 and 5. However, substantial variability exists across workers' ratings, as evidenced by standard deviations greater than 1. Empirically, the three dimensions of the good working life overlapped substantially, with correlations ranging from 0.54 to 0.79 (on a scale from 0 = "no overlap" to 1 = "complete overlap"). However, these correlations also suggest that the overlap was not perfect and that job satisfaction, work meaningfulness, and work psychological richness constitute distinct dimensions of the good working life.
4. *Demographic characteristics are not strongly associated with the good working life*: Workers' demographic background characteristics, including age, sex, education, nationality, and migration background, were only weakly or not significantly associated with each dimension of the good working life in the empirical study conducted for this book, after controlling (or "partialling out") the respective other two dimensions of the good working life.

Older workers reported slightly higher job satisfaction and work psychological richness and slightly lower work meaningfulness scores than younger workers. Women had slightly lower work meaningfulness and slightly higher work psychological richness scores than men, but the two sexes did not differ in terms of job satisfaction. Higher levels of education were associated with slightly higher work meaningfulness but lower job satisfaction, but not work psychological richness. Finally, foreigners reported slightly lower work psychological richness than German citizens.

5. *Workers' personality is differentially associated with the three dimensions of the good working life*: The bright side of workers' personality, as represented by the Big Five characteristics (McCrae & Costa Jr., 1997), core self-evaluations (Judge, 2009), psychological capital (Luthans et al., 2007), and proactive personality (Crant, 1995), had differential associations with the three dimensions of the good working life in the empirical study conducted for this book. The most important personality correlates of job satisfaction were core self-evaluations (e.g., high self-esteem and generalized self-efficacy), emotional stability, and conscientiousness. In contrast, proactive personality, psychological capital, and agreeableness were the best predictors of work meaningfulness. Finally, proactive personality, extraversion, and openness to experience showed the strongest associations with work psychological richness.
6. *Dark personality traits are a double-edged sword with regard to the good working life*: Workers' dark side of personality, represented by the three traits of Machiavellianism, psychopathy, and narcissism (Paulhus & Williams, 2002), was generally negatively related to job satisfaction in the empirical study conducted for this book. In contrast, higher levels of these personality characteristics were associated with higher work psychological richness. Only narcissism was positively related to work meaningfulness. These findings suggest that, although workers with a dark personality are less likely to be satisfied with their jobs, they may also experience occupational well-being in terms of work psychological richness (and for narcissists, higher levels of work meaningfulness).
7. *The possession and use of certain character strengths is associated with higher job satisfaction and work psychological richness, but not work meaningfulness*: The possession and use of certain positive character strengths (Peterson & Seligman, 2004; Ruch et al., 2014) can

contribute to a good working life. Specifically, character strengths associated with the virtues of wisdom/knowledge and justice, as well as select strengths associated with the virtues of courage and transcendence, were linked to higher levels of job satisfaction in the empirical study conducted for this book. The possession and use of character strengths associated with the virtues of humanity and temperance, as well as select strengths from the virtues of wisdom/knowledge, justice, and transcendence, were related to higher work psychological richness. Surprisingly, however, the possession and use of character strengths at work were not significantly related to work meaningfulness.

8. *Workers can create a good working life for themselves through job crafting behaviors*: Job crafting behavior involves proactive attempts to improve the actual and perceived fit between the demands and supplies of one's job with one's personal abilities and needs, respectively (Rudolph et al., 2017; Wrzesniewski & Dutton, 2001). In the empirical study conducted for this book, task crafting, which involves taking on new and challenging (or fewer and less demanding) work projects, was associated with higher job satisfaction. Additionally, task crafting, relational crafting (i.e., improving relationships at work to better fit one's needs), and especially cognitive crafting (i.e., creating a new sense of meaning regarding one's work) were associated with higher work meaningfulness. Finally, all three job crafting dimensions were positively, albeit relatively weakly, associated with work psychological richness, suggesting that workers, through their job crafting behaviors, can proactively make their work more interesting, complex, and perspective changing.
9. *The good working life varies considerably across workers in different industries*: The three dimensions of the good working life varied significantly across workers in the 21 industries represented in the empirical study conducted for this book. The industries with the highest average job satisfaction scores were (a) arts, entertainment, and recreation, (b) accommodation and food service activities, and (c) real estate activities. It seems as if positive emotions related to work are more frequently experienced in these industries. The three industries with the highest average work meaningful scores were (a) water supply, sewerage, waste management, and remediation activities, (b) professional, scientific, and technical activities,

and (c) education. Thus, workers in these industries seem to perceive their work as particularly important and significant for themselves, others, and society at large. Finally, the three industries with the highest average work psychological richness scores were (a) accommodation and food service activities, (b) mining and quarrying, and (c) human health and social work activities. This finding suggests that workers in these industries experience many interesting and complex events as well as a variety of emotions.

10. *Job stressors represent a double-edged sword for the good working life*: The job stressors examined in the empirical study conducted for this book, which were assessed with the Copenhagen Psychosocial Questionnaire (COPSOQ) (Burr et al., 2019; Lincke et al., 2021), were generally negatively related to job satisfaction, mostly positively related to work psychological richness, and mostly non-significantly related to work meaningfulness. Work privacy conflicts, role conflicts, and insecurity over working conditions were particularly strongly linked to lower job satisfaction. In contrast, emotional demands, hiding emotions, dissolution of boundaries between work and nonwork domains, and role conflicts were most strongly related to higher work psychological richness. However, work psychological richness was not significantly related to job insecurity and insecurity over working conditions.
11. *Job resources generally benefit the good working life*: All of the job resources investigated in the empirical study conducted for this book, which were assessed with the COPSOQ instrument (Burr et al., 2019; Lincke et al., 2021), were associated with higher job satisfaction, and most of the job resources were also linked to higher work meaningfulness and work psychological richness, although the latter partial correlations were weaker than those for job satisfaction. Trust and justice, predictability of work, role clarity, support at work, and sense of community were most strongly linked to higher job satisfaction. Quality of leadership, recognition, predictability of work, and feedback were the most important sources of higher work meaningfulness. Finally, influence at work, feedback, and especially possibilities for development were the strongest correlates of higher work psychological richness.
12. *The good working life is related to several positive work outcomes*: In the empirical study conducted for this book, all three dimensions of the good working life were uniquely and positively associated

with job engagement, which represents the physical, emotional, and cognitive energies that workers invest into their work role (Rich et al., 2010). Thus, high levels of job engagement seem to characterize a good working life particularly well. Different dimensions of work performance, including job proficiency, adaptivity, career performance, innovation performance, team performance, and organization performance (Griffin et al., 2007; Welbourne et al., 1998), were positively associated with both job satisfaction and work psychological richness, whereas their links to work meaningfulness were either small or non-significant. Thus, high levels of work performance seem to be not only more satisfying but also make for a more interesting work experience. An exception was job proactivity, which was positively related to both work meaningfulness and psychological richness but not significantly related to job satisfaction. Showing personal initiative at work seems to be linked to viewing one's work as important, growth-oriented, interesting, and complex, but it may not always be a pleasant experience (e.g., it may involve negative feedback and reactance from others, as well as social conflict and energy depletion; Zacher et al., 2019).

13. *Job fatigue is associated with lower job satisfaction but with higher work psychological richness*: The two negative work outcomes in the empirical study conducted for this book, job fatigue and turnover intentions, were strongly associated with lower job satisfaction, and job fatigue was also associated with higher work psychological richness. Thus, satisfying work is less, whereas interesting and complex work is more physically, emotionally, and cognitively depleting for workers. In contrast, work meaningfulness was not significantly associated with either job fatigue or turnover intentions, suggesting that workers who perceive their work as meaningful, on average, do not feel more or less exhausted and are not more or less likely to think about quitting than workers who do not perceive their work as meaningful.
14. *The good working life is associated with the good life in general*: All three dimensions of the good working life were uniquely and positively related to life satisfaction in the empirical study conducted for this book, with job satisfaction being the strongest predictor. In contrast, meaning in life was strongly and positively related to work meaningfulness but only weakly positively related to work psychological richness and even negatively related to job satisfac-

tion. These findings seem to suggest that workers who are satisfied with their jobs may, overall, perceive their life in general as less meaningful. Finally, work psychological richness was strongly and positively related to psychological richness in life in general, whereas job satisfaction and work meaningfulness were non-significant and very weak correlates of psychological richness in life, respectively. These findings suggest that a satisfying and meaningful job does not, in contrast to a psychologically rich job, significantly contribute to a psychologically rich life.

15. *Job satisfaction is positively associated with health and wisdom, whereas work meaningfulness and psychological richness are positively associated with generativity*: Job satisfaction was, by far, the most important contributor to workers' favorable physical and mental health in the empirical study conducted for this book, whereas work meaningfulness and work psychological richness did not play a role in these life outcomes. Moreover, job satisfaction and, very weakly, work psychological richness (but not work meaningfulness) were positively associated with wisdom, which entails deep insights into the human condition and the means and ends of a good life. In terms of important developmental life outcomes, work meaningfulness and work psychological richness, but not job satisfaction, were linked to higher generativity or the concern for establishing and guiding the next generation and contributing to society.

Theoretical Development

The theoretical development of the notion of the good working life and the empirical study conducted for this book are not without limitations, which could be addressed in future research. Table 8.1 summarizes potential implications of the current book for future research on the good working life. In terms of theory development, future research could focus on the nature, antecedents, and consequences of the good working life, as well as mechanisms and boundary conditions of the relations between the good working life and other constructs.

First, it is possible that there are additional dimensions of the good working life that were not considered in this book but may be important to consider in future research (Oishi & Westgate, 2022). Job satisfaction is one indicator of hedonic occupational well-being, and work

Table 8.1 Suggestions for future research: theoretical developments

Topic	*Example research questions*
Nature of the good working life	• Are there additional dimensions of the good working life, such as positive/negative affect or absorption/flow? • Is there a single higher-order good working life factor?
Antecedents of the good working life	• Do the three dimensions of the good working life influence each other reciprocally over time? • Are there additional antecedents of the good working life beyond individual and work characteristics? • How do individual and work characteristics and the three dimensions of the good working life influence each other reciprocally over time?
Consequences of the good working life	• Are there additional consequences beyond job engagement, work performance, turnover intentions, (occupational) health and well-being, as well as generativity and wisdom? • How do the three dimensions of the good working life and important work and life outcomes influence each other reciprocally over time?
Mechanisms and boundary conditions	• Through which mechanisms do individual and work characteristics influence the three dimensions of the good working life? • Through which mechanisms do the three dimensions of the good working life influence important work and life outcomes? • Which individual and contextual factors moderate the associations between the three dimensions of the good working life and their antecedents and consequences?

meaningfulness is one indicator of eudaimonic occupational well-being (Sonnentag, 2015), but certainly, additional indicators of these broad well-being categories exist. For example, future studies could additionally consider the experience of (high levels of) positive affect and (low levels of) negative affect in the work context as further indicators of hedonic occupational well-being (Warr et al., 2014; Watson & Tellegen, 1985). Moreover, indicators of eudaimonic well-being that could be adapted to the work context include perceived autonomy, mastery, personal growth, positive relations with others, and self-acceptance in the work context, which are distinct from work-related purpose or meaningfulness (Ryff, 1989, 1995). There may also be additional well-being dimensions beyond hedonic and eudaimonic occupational well-being and work psychological richness, such as experiencing absorption or flow at work (Csikszentmihalyi, 1997; Peterson et al., 2005). Future research could also consider the question of whether different dimensions of the good working life form a single higher-order factor of the good working life, similar to the general factor of personality (Van der Linden et al., 2021) or the general developmental self-regulation factor (Rauvola & Rudolph, 2023).

Second, future theory development and research could consider how the three dimensions of the good working life influence each other reciprocally over time (regarding the reciprocal relations between job and life satisfaction, see Bialowolski & Weziak-Bialowolska, 2021; Judge & Watanabe, 1993). For example, longitudinal study designs could be used to investigate whether high levels of work meaningfulness and psychological richness predict increases in job satisfaction over time and vice versa. Moreover, future research could explore additional antecedents of the good working life beyond the individual and work-related characteristics examined in this book. Such research could also investigate how individual and work characteristics and the three dimensions of the good working life influence each other reciprocally over time. For example, in line with propositions of action regulation theory (Zacher & Frese, 2018), it may be possible that not only personality characteristics (e.g., psychological capital) predict the good working life, but that living a good working life also leads to changes in workers' personality characteristics over time. Likewise, future theory development and research could identify additional work and life outcomes that result from living a good working life beyond the constructs investigated in this book. Again, such research could also explore reciprocal relations between the good working life and work and life outcomes over time.

Third, I explored partial correlations between various characteristics, outcomes, and the three dimensions of the good working life in this book, but partly due to the lack of relevant theory, I did not examine potential mechanisms and boundary conditions of these associations. Future research could develop a theory on, and empirically investigate, *why*, that is, through which mechanisms, certain individual and work characteristics impact the good working life and *why* the good working life is linked to important work and life outcomes. Moreover, it is likely that the associations identified in this book vary across different individuals and work and life contexts. Thus, future studies could explore how certain individual differences and context factors may moderate (i.e., influence the strength of) associations between the three dimensions of the good working life and other variables.

Methodological Improvements

In terms of methodological improvements, future research on the good working life should consider changes in terms of study participants (i.e., sampling), research designs, measures, and analyses (see Table 8.2).

First, regarding participants and sampling, the study conducted for this book used a large convenience sample of workers from different jobs, organizations, and industries who were recruited and incentivized by a professional online panel provider. Although some of the characteristics of this sample were similar to the characteristics of the working population in Germany (see Chap. 1), the sample was not completely representative of this population (e.g., in terms of education). This lack of complete representativeness does not constitute a problem regarding the research aims of this book, which focused on theoretical generalizability (i.e., supporting theoretical assumptions using a relevant sample) and not sample generalizability (i.e., distributions of characteristics that correspond to the population; Highhouse & Gillespie, 2009). Nevertheless, future studies could aim to recruit more representative samples of workers and explore how individual preferences for each of the three dimensions of the good working life, as well as the actual scores on measures of the good working life, are distributed in such samples. Moreover, participants in the study conducted for this book came from different organizations across Germany. Future research could adopt a multilevel perspective and examine how the good working life differs across and depends on factors that reside at the team, unit, or organizational levels. For example, studies could explore why and under which conditions flexible work arrangements, such as working from home and related developments in the modern workplace driven by increased digitalization (e.g., meeting via videoconference, virtual team collaboration), are associated with the three indicators of the good working life. Lastly, future cross-cultural research could explore how the three dimensions of the good working life vary across different countries and cultural regions and how cultural characteristics, such as individualism/collectivism, power distance, uncertainty avoidance, long-term/short-term future orientation, relate to the good working life (Hofstede, 2001; Knoll et al., 2021).

Second, future studies could explore the good working life using different and more rigorous research designs than cross-sectional surveys. The cross-sectional design of the study conducted for this book neither allows conclusions about temporal stability of, or changes in, the focal variables

Table 8.2 Suggestions for future research: methodological improvements

Topic	*Example research questions*
Participants	• How are individual preferences for, and actual scores on, the three dimensions of the good working life distributed in representative worker samples? • How does the good working life vary across different organizations? • How does the good working life vary across different countries?
Research design	• How and why do the three dimensions of the good working life change "within" workers and relate to each other over time in longitudinal studies? • How and why do the three dimensions of the good working life fluctuate "within" workers across short time span in experience sampling or daily diary studies? • How can the good working life (or its predictors) be enhanced through randomized controlled interventions? • What is workers' understanding of the meaning of the good working life, and how do their personal narratives of the good working life vary and change over time in qualitative studies?
Measures	• Which self-report measures of the three dimensions of the good working life are most reliable, valid, and practical? • Are there more objective measures of the good working life that do not suffer from the limitations of self-reports?
Analyses	• How can the good working life be analyzed across multiple levels (e.g., within persons over time, between persons, team, organization, country)? • How do the three dimensions of the good working life interact in predicting important outcomes, or form latent profiles? • How does the (mis-)fit between workers' preferred and their actual working life predict important work and life outcomes?

over time, nor about causality among the variables (Spector, 2019). Longitudinal studies with three or ideally more measurement waves could examine how and why the three dimensions of the good working life change "within" workers and relate to each other over time (Ployhart & Vandenberg, 2010; Wang et al., 2017). For example, such research could examine whether certain work or life events lead to changes in the good working life over time. Likewise, experience sampling or diary studies could investigate how and why the three dimensions of the good working life fluctuate or vary "within" workers across relatively short time spans, such as hours, days, or weeks (Beal, 2015; Gabriel et al., 2019). Indeed, research showed that substantial amounts of variance (i.e., approximately

40%) in job satisfaction reside at the within-person level (McCormick et al., 2020; Podsakoff et al., 2019). Both longitudinal and experience sampling designs could further be combined with intervention designs in which research attempts to manipulate certain independent variables and observe how the good working life dimensions as dependent variables change over time; or studies could manipulate the good working life itself and observe the consequences for other work and life outcomes over time. Importantly, such designs require random assignment of participants to a neutral control group in which the independent variable is not changed. Lastly, future research could also use qualitative research methods (Wilhelmy & Köhler, 2022), such as interviews, to explore workers' lived experiences, understanding, and personal narratives and meanings of the good working life over time.

Third, all constructs in the study conducted for this book were assessed by self-report, which may lead to potential problems, such as self-enhancement bias, social desirability bias, or common method bias (Podsakoff et al., 2012; Spector, 1994). However, artificially inflated correlations may be less of a concern given that, for each association with a dimension of the good working life, I controlled for the respective other two dimensions and, thus, partialled out the variance explained by these constructs. Nevertheless, future studies should attempt to identify those self-report measures of the three dimensions of the good working life that are most reliable, well validated, and practical (i.e., relatively short for use in longitudinal survey studies or in organizational practice). Additionally, future studies could try to collect data from different sources (e.g., archival data or observer ratings of work characteristics, coworker and supervisor ratings of work outcomes) in addition to self-reports of the three dimensions of the good working life, which arguably represent subjective constructs that require workers stating their opinions. Nevertheless, future research could explore whether there are measures of the good working life that do not suffer from the limitations of self-report questionnaires, such as questions in qualitative interviews, field observations, or reports from close friends or family members.

Future studies with more sophisticated theoretical backgrounds, research designs, and measures need to consider how the good working life and its links with other constructs should be analyzed. When data are collected at and analyzed within and across multiple levels, such as within persons over time in longitudinal or experience sampling studies or at the team, organizational, or country levels, multilevel analyses are required

(Bliese et al., 2007). Other analytical possibilities include the consideration of interactions among the three dimensions of the good working life, as well as latent profile analyses that focus on certain constellations or "types" regarding the combination of scores on the dimensions (Spurk et al., 2020). Such latent profiles could be linked to similar antecedents and consequences as those investigated in the current book, and research could also explore how and why such good working life profiles may change over time using latent transition analyses. Finally, future studies could use polynomial regression analyses with response surface plots (Humberg et al., 2019; Yao & Ma, 2023) to examine how the fit (or congruence) and misfit (or incongruence) between workers' preferred good working life (e.g., a preference for the psychologically rich working life vs. the satisfied and meaningful working lives) and their actual good working life relates to important work and life outcomes. For instance, workers who prefer a psychologically rich working life but do not actually experience psychological richness at work might experience lower job engagement than workers whose actual working life matches their preferences.

Practical Recommendations for Workers

Based on the insights into the good working life presented in this book, several practical recommendations for individual workers, leaders, and organizations can be derived. These recommendations are summarized in Table 8.3.

Based on the insights of this book, workers could regularly remind themselves that the occupational well-being is more than high levels of job satisfaction and that the good working life also includes work meaningfulness and work psychological richness as key dimensions. People's working lives may not always be satisfying, but that does not necessarily mean that their occupational well-being is low; they may be leading a meaningful or psychologically rich working life. In this regard, it also seems important for workers to reflect on their personal preferences regarding the three dimensions of the good working life, their actual working life, and how a potential misfit between their preferred and their actual working life could be managed, such that these lives become better aligned. Moreover, as shown in this book, each dimension of the good working life comes with certain benefits but also certain costs or downsides that need to be managed. For example, a psychologically rich working life is associated with

Table 8.3 Recommendations for practice

Topic	*Practical examples*
Workers	
Different dimensions of occupational well-being	Workers could consider that occupational well-being is more than just job satisfaction but also includes work meaningfulness and work psychological richness.
Preferred working life	Workers could reflect on the fit or misfit between their preferred working life and their actual working life and think about how these two lives could be better aligned.
Use of character strengths and job crafting	Workers could make use of their character strengths and certain job crafting behaviors to enhance the three dimensions of the good working life.
Effects on important life outcomes	Workers could remind themselves of the beneficial effects of the good working life dimensions on important life outcomes, such as life satisfaction, physical and mental health, as well as generativity and wisdom.
Leaders	
Consider workers' individual differences	Leaders could take workers' individual differences in personality into account when planning interventions to improve occupational well-being.
Work design I: reducing job stressors	Leaders could reduce stressors to improve job satisfaction; if reducing stressors is not possible, they could remind workers about the positive effects of stressors on work psychological richness.
Work design II: increasing job resources	Leaders could increase job resources to improve all dimensions of the good working life; some job resources are more relevant for certain dimensions of the good working life than others.
Organizations	
Facilitate the good working life for important work outcomes	Organizations could conduct interventions to facilitate the good working life to improve important work outcomes, such as job engagement and performance, and to reduce fatigue and turnover intentions.
Offer training and development opportunities regarding the good working life	Organizations could offer training and development opportunities to enhance certain antecedents (e.g., psychological capital, use of character strengths, job crafting) of the good working life.
Consider industry differences in the good working life	Organizations could conduct interventions to target dimensions of the good working life that tend to be low in their respective industry.

more job stressors and higher job fatigue, whereas job satisfaction is related to lower meaning in life.

Two individual, proactive approaches that may help enhance the three dimensions of the good working life are the use of actually available character strengths and job crafting behaviors. For instance, workers could use task crafting (e.g., asking for a more challenging project and asking to reduce demands) to improve their job satisfaction. Alternatively, they could engage in cognitive crafting to enhance work meaningfulness. Finally, the use of character strengths and job crafting could be increased if workers regularly remind themselves of the beneficial effects of the good working life dimensions on various important life outcomes, such as life satisfaction, physical and mental health, as well as generativity and wisdom.

Practical Recommendations for Leaders

Organizational leaders and supervisors hold responsibility for their employees' occupational health, well-being, and safety and, thus, should also familiarize themselves with the notion of the good working life and how to enhance it. First, leaders should consider workers' individual differences, especially in terms of preferences for certain dimensions of the good working life and personality characteristics, when planning and conducting interventions to improve occupational well-being. Not every worker is equally likely to respond favorably to interventions designed to enhance job satisfaction, possibly because they are more interested in the meaningful or the psychologically rich working life. Furthermore, leaders are important agents when it comes to improving occupational health and well-being through work design (Wegge et al., 2014). On the one hand, leaders could reduce key job stressors, such as quantitative and emotional demands, role conflicts, and uncertainty over working conditions, to improve job satisfaction. However, if reducing job stressors is not possible, leaders could remind workers about the positive effects of stressors on work psychological richness. On the other hand, leaders could design work by increasing important job resources, such as possibilities for development, role clarity, influence at work and, importantly, the quality of leadership, which involves clear and empowering interactions with their employees (Rudolph et al., 2022).

Practical Recommendations for Organizations

There are also a number of ways to enhance the good working life among individual workers through activities at the organizational level, which includes companies' executive leadership and human resource management. First of all, however, organizations should develop a shared understanding among their leaders and workers that the dimensions of the good working life are associated with various important work outcomes, including job engagement, performance and, especially for job satisfaction, reduced fatigue and turnover intentions. Such a shared understanding can motivate efforts at all organizational levels to support individuals' good working lives. More specifically, organizations should offer workers training and development opportunities that aim to enhance the good working life dimensions directly by improving occupational well-being or indirectly by targeting the antecedents of occupational well-being. For example, training programs that focus on developing workers' core self-evaluations, psychological capital, their use of character strengths, or their job crafting behaviors have been shown to be effective (Harzer & Ruch, 2013; Judge, 2009; Lupşa et al., 2020; Oprea et al., 2019). Finally, organizations should take note of the industry differences identified in the study conducted for this book and target interventions at those dimensions of the good working life that tend to be relatively lower in their respective industry.

Summary

The good working life represents a new and useful concept for workers, leaders, and organizations. Inspired by research in the fields of positive psychology and work and organizational psychology, in this book, I presented the results of a large-scale empirical study on the potential antecedents and consequences of the good working life. I hope the findings will inspire further research on this exciting concept and evidence-based applications in organizations.

References

Beal, D. J. (2015). ESM 2.0: State of the art and future potential of experience sampling methods in organizational research. *Annual Review of Organizational Psychology and Organizational Behavior*, *2*(1), 383–407. https://doi.org/10.1146/annurev-orgpsych-032414-111335

Bialowolski, P., & Weziak-Bialowolska, D. (2021). Longitudinal evidence for reciprocal effects Between life satisfaction and job satisfaction. *Journal of Happiness Studies, 22*, 1287–1312. https://doi.org/10.1007/s10902-020-00273-1

Bliese, P. D., Chan, D., & Ployhart, R. E. (2007). Multilevel methods: Future directions in measurement, longitudinal analyses, and nonnormal outcomes. *Organizational Research Methods, 10*(4), 551–563. https://doi.org/10.1177/1094428107301102

Burr, H., Berthelsen, H., Moncada, S., Nübling, M., Dupret, E., Demiral, Y., et al. (2019). The third version of the Copenhagen psychosocial questionnaire. *Safety and Health at Work, 10*(4), 482–503. https://doi.org/10.1016/j.shaw.2019.10.002

Crant, J. M. (1995). The Proactive Personality Scale and objective job performance among real estate agents. *Journal of Applied Psychology, 80*(4), 532–537. https://doi.org/10.1037/0021-9010.80.4.532

Csikszentmihalyi, M. (1997). *Finding flow: The psychology of engagement with everyday life*. Basic Books.

Gabriel, A. S., Podsakoff, N. P., Beal, D. J., Scott, B. A., Sonnentag, S., Trougakos, J. P., & Butts, M. M. (2019). Experience sampling methodology: A discussion of critical trends and considerations for scholarly advancement. *Organizational Research Methods, 22*(4), 969–1006. https://doi.org/10.1177/1094428118802626

Griffin, M. A., Neal, A., & Parker, S. K. (2007). A new model of work role performance: Positive behavior in uncertain and interdependent contexts. *Academy of Management Journal, 50*, 327–347. https://doi.org/10.5465/AMJ.2007.24634438

Harzer, C., & Ruch, W. (2013). The application of signature character strengths and positive experiences at work. *Journal of Happiness Studies, 14*(3), 965–983. https://doi.org/10.1007/s10902-012-9364-0

Highhouse, S., & Gillespie, J. Z. (2009). Do samples really matter that much? In C. E. Lance & R. J. Vandenberg (Eds.), *Statistical and methodological myths and urban legends: Doctrine, verity and fable in the organizational and social sciences* (pp. 247–265). Routledge.

Hofstede, G. (2001). *Culture's consequences: Comparing values, behaviors, institutions, and organizations across nations*. Sage.

Humberg, S., Nestler, S., & Back, M. D. (2019). Response surface analysis in personality and social psychology: Checklist and clarifications for the case of congruence hypotheses. *Social Psychological and Personality Science, 10*(3), 409–419. https://doi.org/10.1177/1948550618757600

Judge, T., & Watanabe, S. (1993). Another look at the job satisfaction-life satisfaction relationship. *Journal of Applied Psychology, 78*(6), 939–948. https://doi.org/10.1037/0021-9010.78.6.939

Judge, T. A. (2009). Core self-evaluations and work success. *Current Directions in Psychological Science, 18*(1), 58–62. https://doi.org/10.1111/j.1467-8721.2009.01606.x

Judge, T. A., Locke, E. A., Durham, C. C., & Kluger, A. N. (1998). Dispositional effects on job and life satisfaction: The role of core evaluations. *Journal of Applied Psychology, 83*(1), 17–34. https://doi.org/10.1037/0021-9010.83.1.17

Knoll, M., Götz, M., Adriasola, E., Al-Atwi, A. A., Arenas, A., Atitsogbe, K. A., et al. (2021). International differences in employee silence motives: Scale validation, prevalence, and relationships with culture characteristics across 33 countries. *Journal of Organizational Behavior, 42*(5), 619–648. https://doi.org/10.1002/job.2512

Lincke, H. J., Vomstein, M., Lindner, A., Nolle, I., Häberle, N., Haug, A., & Nübling, M. (2021). COPSOQ III in Germany: Validation of a standard instrument to measure psychosocial factors at work. *Journal of Occupational Medicine and Toxicology, 16*, 1–15. https://doi.org/10.1186/s12995-021-00331-1

Locke, E. A. (1976). The nature and causes of job satisfaction. In M. D. Dunnette (Ed.), *Handbook of industrial and organizational psychology* (pp. 1297–1349). Rand McNally.

Lupşa, D., Vîrga, D., Maricuţoiu, L. P., & Rusu, A. (2020). Increasing psychological capital: A pre-registered meta-analysis of controlled interventions. *Applied Psychology, 69*(4), 1506–1556. https://doi.org/10.1111/apps.12219

Luthans, F., Avolio, B. J., Avey, J. B., & Norman, S. M. (2007). Positive psychological capital: Measurement and relationship with performance and satisfaction. *Personnel Psychology, 60*(3), 541–572. https://doi.org/10.1111/j.1744-6570.2007.00083.x

McCormick, B. W., Reeves, C. J., Downes, P. E., Li, N., & Ilies, R. (2020). Scientific contributions of within-person research in management: Making the juice worth the squeeze. *Journal of Management, 46*(2), 321–350. https://doi.org/10.1177/0149206318788435

McCrae, R. R., & Costa, P. T., Jr. (1997). Personality trait structure as a human universal. *American Psychologist, 52*(5), 509–516. https://doi.org/10.1037/0003-066X.52.5.509

Oishi, S., Choi, H., Buttrick, N., Heintzelman, S. J., Kushlev, K., Westgate, E. C., et al. (2019). The psychologically rich life questionnaire. *Journal of Research in Personality, 81*, 257–270. https://doi.org/10.1016/j.jrp.2019.06.010

Oishi, S., & Westgate, E. C. (2022). A psychologically rich life: Beyond happiness and meaning. *Psychological Review, 129*(4), 790–811. https://doi.org/10.1037/rev0000317

Oprea, B. T., Barzin, L., Vîrgă, D., Iliescu, D., & Rusu, A. (2019). Effectiveness of job crafting interventions: A meta-analysis and utility analysis. *European*

Journal of Work and Organizational Psychology, 28(6), 723–741. https://doi.org/10.1080/1359432X.2019.1646728

Paulhus, D. L., & Williams, K. M. (2002). The dark triad of personality: Narcissism, Machiavellianism, and psychopathy. *Journal of Research in Personality, 36*(6), 556–563. https://doi.org/10.1016/S0092-6566(02)00505-6

Peterson, C., Park, N., & Seligman, M. E. P. (2005). Orientations to happiness and life satisfaction: The full versus the empty life. *Journal of Happiness Studies, 6*(25–41). https://doi.org/10.1007/s10902-004-1278-z

Peterson, C., & Seligman, M. E. P. (2004). *Character strengths and virtues: A handbook and classification*. American Psychological Association.

Ployhart, R. E., & Vandenberg, R. J. (2010). Longitudinal research: The theory, design, and analysis of change. *Journal of Management, 36*(1), 94–120. https://doi.org/10.1177/0149206309352110

Podsakoff, N. P., Spoelma, T. M., Chawla, N., & Gabriel, A. S. (2019). What predicts within-person variance in applied psychology constructs? An empirical examination. *Journal of Applied Psychology, 104*(6), 727–754. https://doi.org/10.1037/apl0000374

Podsakoff, P. M., MacKenzie, S. B., & Podsakoff, N. P. (2012). Sources of method bias in social science research and recommendation on how to control it. *Annual Review of Psychology, 63*, 539–569. https://doi.org/10.1146/annurev-psych-120710-100452

Rauvola, R. S., & Rudolph, C. W. (2023). An operational integration of lifespan development theories. *Current Psychology, 42*, 11184–11194. https://doi.org/10.1007/s12144-021-02385-0

Rich, B. L., LePine, J. A., & Crawford, E. A. (2010). Job engagement: Antecedents and effects on job performance. *Academy of Management Journal, 53*(3), 617–635. https://doi.org/10.5465/AMJ.2010.51468988

Ruch, W., Martínez-Martí, M. L., Proyer, R. T., & Harzer, C. (2014). The Character Strengths Rating Form (CSRF): Development and initial assessment of a 24-item rating scale to assess character strengths. *Personality and Individual Differences, 68*, 53–58. https://doi.org/10.1016/j.paid.2014.03.042

Rudolph, C. W., Breevaart, K., & Zacher, H. (2022). Disentangling between-person and reciprocal within-person relationships between perceived leadership and employee wellbeing. *Journal of Occupational Health Psychology, 27*(4), 441–450. https://doi.org/10.1037/ocp0000320

Rudolph, C. W., Katz, I. M., Lavigne, K. N., & Zacher, H. (2017). Job crafting: A meta-analysis of relationships with individual differences, job characteristics, and work outcomes. *Journal of Vocational Behavior, 102*, 112–138. https://doi.org/10.1016/j.jvb.2017.05.008

Ryff, C. D. (1989). Happiness is everything, or is it? Explorations on the meaning of psychological well-being. *Journal of Personality and Social Psychology, 57*(6), 1069–1081. https://doi.org/10.1037/0022-3514.57.6.1069

Ryff, C. D. (1995). Psychological well-being in adult life. *Current Directions in Psychological Science, 4*(4), 99–104. https://doi.org/10.1111/1467-8721.ep10772395

Sonnentag, S. (2015). Dynamics of well-being. *Annual Review of Organizational Psychology and Organizational Behavior, 2*, 261–293. https://doi.org/10.1146/annurev-orgpsych-032414-111347

Spector, P. E. (1994). Using self-report questionnaires in OB research: A comment on the use of a controversial method. *Journal of Organizational Behavior, 15*, 385–392. https://doi.org/10.1002/job.4030150503

Spector, P. E. (2019). Do not cross me: Optimizing the use of cross-sectional designs. *Journal of Business and Psychology, 34*(2), 125–137. https://doi.org/10.1007/s10869-018-09613-8

Spurk, D., Hirschi, A., Wang, M., Valero, D., & Kauffeld, S. (2020). Latent profile analysis: A review and "how to" guide of its application within vocational behavior research. *Journal of Vocational Behavior, 120*, 103445. https://doi.org/10.1016/j.jvb.2020.103445

Steger, M. F., Dik, B. J., & Duffy, R. D. (2012). Measuring meaningful work: The work and meaning inventory (WAMI). *Journal of Career Assessment, 20*(3), 322–337. https://doi.org/10.1177/1069072711436160

Van der Linden, D., Dunkel, C. S., & Wu, P. (2021). Is there a meaningful general factor of personality? *Spanish Journal of Psychology, 24*, e9. https://doi.org/10.1017/SJP.2021.2

Wang, M., Beal, D. J., Chan, D., Newman, D. A., Vancouver, J. B., & Vandenberg, R. J. (2017). Longitudinal research: A panel discussion on conceptual issues, research design, and statistical techniques. *Work, Aging and Retirement, 3*(1), 1–24. https://doi.org/10.1093/workar/waw033

Warr, P., Bindl, U. K., Parker, S. K., & Inceoglu, I. (2014). Four-quadrant investigation of job-related affects and behaviours. *European Journal of Work and Organizational Psychology, 23*(3), 342–363. https://doi.org/10.1080/1359432X.2012.744449

Watson, D., & Tellegen, A. (1985). Toward a consensual structure of mood. *Psychological Bulletin, 98*(2), 219–235. https://doi.org/10.1037/0033-2909.98.2.219

Wegge, J., Shemla, M., & Haslam, S. A. (2014). Leader behavior as a determinant of health at work: Specification and evidence of five key pathways. *German Journal of Human Resource Management, 28*(1-2), 6–23. https://doi.org/10.1177/239700221402800102

Welbourne, T. M., Johnson, D. E., & Erez, A. (1998). The role-based performance scale: Validity analysis of a theory-based measure. *Academy of Management Journal, 41*(5), 540–555. https://doi.org/10.2307/256941

Wilhelmy, A., & Köhler, T. (2022). Qualitative research in work and organizational psychology journals: Practices and future opportunities. *European*

Journal of Work and Organizational Psychology, 31(2), 161–185. https://doi.org/10.1080/1359432X.2021.2009457

Wrzesniewski, A., & Dutton, J. E. (2001). Crafting a job: Revisioning employees as active crafters of their work. *Academy of Management Review, 26*(2), 179–201. https://doi.org/10.5465/AMR.2001.4378011

Yao, Y. A., & Ma, Z. (2023). Toward a holistic perspective of congruence research with the polynomial regression model. *Journal of Applied Psychology, 108*(3), 446–465. https://doi.org/10.1037/apl0001028

Zacher, H., & Baumeister, R. F. (2024). Differences among a satisfied, a meaningful, and a psychologically rich working life. *Journal of Positive Psychology.* https://doi.org/10.1080/17439760.2024.2417102

Zacher, H., & Frese, M. (2018). Action regulation theory: Foundations, current knowledge, and future directions. In D. S. Ones, N. R. Anderson, C. Viswesvaran, & H. K. Sinangil (Eds.), *The SAGE handbook of industrial, work and organizational psychology (2nd ed.), Vol. 2: Organizational psychology* (pp. 80–102). Sage.

Zacher, H., Schmitt, A., Jimmieson, N. L., & Rudolph, C. W. (2019). Dynamic effects of personal initiative on engagement and exhaustion: The role of mood, autonomy, and support. *Journal of Organizational Behavior, 40*(1), 38–58. https://doi.org/10.1002/job.2277

Index

H. Zacher, *The Good Working Life*,
https://doi.org/10.1007/978-3-031-77221-4

The manufacturer's authorised representative in the EU is Springer Nature Customer Service Centre GmbH, Europaplatz 3, 69115 Heidelberg, Germany. If you have any concerns regarding our products, please contact ProductSafety@springernature.com

Printed and bound by CPI Group (UK) Ltd, Croydon, CR0 4YY
30/09/2026
02225609-0007